RELENTLESS

12 ROUNDS TO SUCCESS

EDDIE HEARN

HODDER

First published in Great Britain in 2020 by Hodder & Stoughton
An Hachette UK company

This paperback edition published in 2022

2

With Matt Whyman

A CIP catalogue record for this title is available from the British Library

Paperback ISBN 9781529312232
eBook ISBN 9781529312218

Typeset in Adobe Garamond by Palimpsest Book Production Limited, Falkirk, Stirlingshire

Printed and bound in Great Britain by Clays Ltd, Elcograf S.p.A.

Hodder & Stoughton policy is to use papers that are natural,
renewable and recyclable products and made from wood grown in sustainable
forests. The logging and manufacturing processes are expected to conform to the
environmental regulations of the country of origin.

Hodder & Stoughton Ltd
Carmelite House
50 Victoria Embankment
London EC4Y 0DZ

www.hodder.co.uk

To my beautiful wife, Chloe, and my amazing children, Isabella and Sophia, the driving force behind my success.

Dad, you get enough mentions in here!
Mum, all my greatest qualities come from you.

Nanny Joan, I know you will be enjoying this one up there.

CONTENTS

INTRODUCTION

I have to be honest. I still can't believe I've been asked to write a book of this kind. I could possibly understand a boxing book – the big fights, the controversy, the drama behind the scenes – but this one is very different. This is my attempt to sum up what I have learned from my life and career, and how it may help you on your own journey. It explains how I pursued my dreams with drive and determination, while I attempted to carve out a name in my own right and come out on top.

Unfortunately, I can't give you a story about how I made it out of a council estate from nothing (that's one for my old man). What I can offer, however, is an insight into my mindset and work ethic and an honest account of key moments throughout my career, which have ultimately led to changing the face of boxing.

It may surprise you to know that I don't think I am particularly gifted. I'm definitely my own biggest critic. I rarely admire my work and always think there is room for improvement. What I do have, though, is a strange addiction to succeed, to push boundaries and to prove people wrong. My work ethic is relentless and, as you'll discover throughout the book, this is the most important quality that you can have.

This book is split into two parts. I will start with a little detail on my background and upbringing, which I feel has played a major role in shaping who I am, and is where my mindset and drive came from. I didn't want this to be a biography, but at times it is helpful to recap my backstory and the pivotal moments in my life. In the second part, I'll take you through some of the big moments in my career that have taught me the fundamental skills required for success. You'll learn about the importance of selling and negotiating, having the right drive and energy, finding passion in your work, and a lot more.

I've had the honour of being a part of some of the biggest fights in boxing history and working with some of the best fighters in the game, but I can't mention all of them here. Instead, I'll look back at some of the events that have taught me valuable lessons in life, and the ones that provide an insight into how you can achieve your goals.

I can't say for certain that every lesson is going to be right for you, or that this book will revolutionise your business, but I hope you will find some inspiration here that drives you forward. My purpose is to focus your mind and keep you sane during challenging moments ahead, because when you are working towards your objectives, there will be tough times that you need to battle through.

As I started putting pen to paper, the world started to change considerably. Now, more than ever, a relentless work ethic – alongside solid business fundamentals and a balanced mind – is essential if we are to ride this out. The global pandemic has thrown shade on what we may previously have felt was important. I think I speak for many when I say that we now appreciate happiness as much as success, and the two may not be linked as closely as we once thought. Like many others, I may have been guilty of being too single-minded over the years, and too focused on 'success' over happiness, self-satisfaction and purpose.

As the world starts to return to some kind of normality, it is nearly time to go again. Only this time, we need to fight even harder. Everything has changed and you need to be prepared for a bumpy road ahead.

I hope you enjoy the book and that it can help bring you success. But first, you have to establish what success really is and what it means to you – what it is you want to achieve in your life and career.

As the years roll by, you begin to realise that what you thought may have been considered a success, really wasn't. Success, for me, is the feeling of purpose that leads to fulfilment. It's the passion of loving what you do. I don't think I have half the answers yet, but I hope by writing this book I can help you (and, in a way, myself) continue the journey to 'success' and happiness.

Part One

HOW I STARTED

Round 1

NO QUARTER

Growing up, I had everything, but I was always Barry Hearn's son.

I also had a devoted father, with no time for privilege or head starts in life, which made me who I am today. We lived in a big house outside Brentwood in Essex. Today, it's the Matchroom headquarters. Back then it was the family home.

I was five years old when we moved there from Ongar, heading east from London and moving up in the world. Mascalls was a sprawling estate that looked out towards the capital's skyline. With pillars at the entrance, a lot of rooms, and thirteen thousand square feet going out into the gardens, it was the first time I had that feeling you get when you have something special. I knew it set us apart from most people, but the one thing I cared about more than anything else was not wealth, it was sport.

'Is Dad home tonight?' I'd ask my mum, because more often than not his work meant that he would be away.

If he was due back, then usually it would be in time for tea. Together with my older sister, Katie, we were one of those old-school families who placed great importance in eating meals together. If I knew Dad was going to be home,

I'd sit on the stairs by the window overlooking the drive and wait for him. From the quiet country lane beyond, I learned to recognise the sound of his car engine coming up the hill. I remember the excitement with which I'd greet the sight of his car as it turned through the gates. Dad drove a white Mercedes, which was unmistakeable in so many ways. Not least on account of the personalised number plate: THE 147S.

'Dad, can we play cricket now? Can we, Dad? Can we?'

Like any kid, I was pestering for attention before my old man even stepped through the door. Dad always looked sharp and had a smile on his face. Given how hard he worked and how often he was away, he probably came home absolutely knackered and hoping to put his feet up. I imagine my attention was the last thing he needed, and yet his reaction to seeing me was always the same. Being a parent now, I know how hard it is when the tank is empty.

'Course we can, son! Just let me get changed and I'll meet you out there.'

I would always be ready. When it came to knocking a cricket ball around with my dad, I needed all the gear for good reason. With my gloves and pads on, ball in my pocket and bat in hand, I'd be out there waiting for him on the lawn. Dad would join me soon afterwards, dressed down for the remains of a day that was far from over through his eyes. While other fathers might have headed straight for the dinner table or a pint, he'd come outside to spend time with me, and give me his full attention.

'I'm ready,' I'd say, taking up position in front of the wicket I had put together earlier. I'd toss Dad the cricket ball and he would start to mark out his run-up. With my eyes on him, I'd tap my bat to the ground in preparation. The grass was worn down in a stripe here, because this was the spot we would always use. It was a ritual in many ways, and also a rite of passage.

'Okay, Silver Spoon,' he'd reply, which was his nickname for me. 'Let's see what you got.'

The moment my dad sized me up, turned and took several paces back, I knew that I couldn't afford to let my concentration lapse. I'd watch him come back around and begin his run-up, and without blinking, I'd tighten my grip around the bat. All I ever wanted was to make him proud and hear the words, 'Great shot!' Thirty years on, nothing has changed. We're still as competitive as ever and it's a trait he's instilled in me and in business. It's his ethos, in that you don't get given anything.

Every time, without fail, and from the very first time we played together, my dad would bowl at full tilt. He never eased me into the game and he was good at cricket – instead he treated me like a competitor. All of that stuff about letting your children enjoy an easy win? Not on his turf: Dad didn't believe in it.

In facing the full force of my dad's bowling, I soon realised there was only one way to respond to it. Flinching, ducking or dodging out of the way got me nowhere. If I wanted to see results, my only option was to face him head on and aim to tank him all over the garden. It was a hit-and-miss process, and painful on occasions, but over time I learned to rise to the challenge.

It wasn't difficult to see when Dad was proud of me – he would always let me know. It was almost as if the more I carted him around the garden, the happier he was. Even though it would take him a couple of minutes to fetch the ball.

As my game improved, my dad spent more time retrieving

the ball than bowling at me, but not once did his enthusiasm fade. We wouldn't stop until it got dark or Mum called us in for dinner.

It's only when you look back on your childhood that you appreciate what your parents were trying to do for you. My dad's approach to me might seem unconventional, but it worked. He was terrified that I'd grow up to become all the things he didn't like – the spoilt rich kid having things handed to him on a plate. On account of the huge success he'd enjoyed, I could easily have had all that. We lived in a giant house with a pool and fancy cars in the drive, which is why he went to great lengths to bring me up in a way that he considered to be right and proper. I was his project. A work in progress that he'd probably tell you is still ongoing.

All I know is that I owe him a great deal for the experience. Everything he did as a parent came down to making sure that I never, ever expected opportunities to come to me. If I wanted to get on in life, and truly make my mark, then I would have to work hard. Ultimately, I'd have to make sacrifices in pursuit of excellence.

You could say that Dad was busy making sacrifices when I was born. On 8 June 1979, he missed my arrival in hospital because he was playing a best of three at Romford snooker club. On that day, while Mum cursed his absence through the contractions, Dad was 1–1 with Crunchy Warn, a hall regular, and no consideration was given to leaving the game until it was through.

'Barry,' said the guy who answered the phone at the hall. 'It's the hospital – the baby's on its way!'

'It'll have to wait.' Dad instructed the poor guy to reply. 'There's fifty quid riding on this.'

For my father, a working-class man with a competitive spirit and big ambitions, there was simply too much at stake here. But it meant more than fifty quid – he had to get the win. It wasn't a heartless decision for him to take, but a matter of principle. Maybe it was his lucky day, because he didn't just become a father for the second time, but he won the match as well. Afterwards, with the cash in his pocket, he raced across to the hospital where mother and child awaited him.

'You bastard!' Mum was sitting up in bed with a face on, clutching me protectively. 'How could you miss the birth of your own son?'

My parents, Barry and Susan, are a tight couple. They fight all the time, but love each other to pieces. It's just how they are. They're one of those couples that bring different qualities to their marriage, and it just fits.

Mum is proper old school, careful with money – she'd walk an extra two miles to get ten pence off a carton of milk. Dad is the complete opposite to her. He isn't frivolous, but deeply generous and occasionally reckless. He's earned his wealth the hard way, having come from nothing, and uses it to enjoy life. I started from a completely different place, and yet thanks to Mum and Dad, I shared the same grounding: everything is out there, but nothing comes easy and there is no substitute for hard work.

Born and raised in Dagenham, Dad watched his own father work five days a week driving buses around East London, and then come home to switch off. That was my grandad's life, which pretty much amounted to earning a wage to put food on the table, and keep a roof over the family, with some left over to spend on cigarettes. There was no ambition, no drive. A sense of contentment with my grandmother, perhaps, but a life that didn't chime with Dad. In some ways, it was what motivated him to get out there and make his mark on the world that his own father didn't.

By his own admission, Dad was a 'Jack the lad'; a bit of a Del Boy with an eye for ventures that would make him some money. Growing up, he was always ducking and diving to make a living.

At the same time, he found he was decent with figures and went down the route of qualifying as one of the country's youngest chartered accountants. It was a move into a traditional career that didn't last long, though. Dad was so hungry to keep pushing and grab the opportunities, which explains how he made the switch from processing tax returns to working as a finance director for an investment company that owned a major textile design company. They put him on a salary and then offered him a percentage if he could identify any ventures with growth potential. That's how snooker came into his life in a big way, and he never looked back.

In the seventies, snooker halls could always rely on regulars to keep them in business. When the opportunity arose for Dad to buy one in Romford, he did so mainly as a property investment. I'm sure it helped that he liked to play, and it gave him a chance to mix business with pleasure, but it was a smart move. At the time, with colour television just starting out, the BBC demonstrated the new technology by airing the World Snooker Championships. It proved to be popular, and as the sport began to grow, Dad knew he was onto a winner.

He began by developing the snooker hall business all over the south of England under the chain name Lucania, as well as fruit machine businesses in the East End of London. His favourite club in Romford, called The Matchroom, also housed his office. Dad was tucked away under the main hall, so it meant he was never more than a flight of steps from the action.

One day, working at his desk, Dad picked up the phone to the club manager.

'Barry, you got to come upstairs and see this kid play,' said the guy with some excitement. 'He's unbelievable!'

So, Dad left his office and trudged upstairs to the main hall. Through the low lights and the cigarette smoke, he saw the punters crowding around one table, There, this beanpole ginger lad was preparing to cue up a shot. My dad found a space and watched a young genius at work potting ball after ball. Moments after he cleared the table, Dad had his arm around the lad's shoulder, inviting him to the office for a business chat.

'How old are you, kid?'

'Eighteen.'

'What's your name?' my dad asked.

'Steve,' he told him. 'Steve Davis.'

My dad has a nose for opportunity, and he could see this working-class young man was magic. They started talking, and without knowing exactly what he was doing, Dad offered him a spot in the Lucania Annual Snooker Championships. It was literally a reaction to seeing the man light up the baize and proved to be one of his soundest investments.

From there on out, like two cowboys in the Wild West, Dad and Steve toured snooker halls around the country to hustle players. They went everywhere, from Lincoln to Torquay. My dad would walk in, gesture at the lanky, quiet, awkward-looking lad with him, and say, 'I've got this lad and I guarantee he'll beat anyone willing to take him on.' Naturally, people would size up Steve, see an easy win for themselves, and offer up their club captain with five hundred quid at stake. Dad would accept all wagers, and then stand back as the future six-time world snooker champion schooled them.

Several frames later, with the victory in his pocket and people gawping in shock at what they had witnessed, Steve would wait nervously for my dad to collect their winnings before they quite literally ran for it. They made a great team, to be honest, and Dad worked hard to build up his young player's reputation. Over time, in those halls, Steve took on legends such as Alex Higgins and Ray Reardon, and proved to be so devastating that he inspired respect, admiration and near-legendary status.

During this time, towards the late seventies, snooker exploded in popularity. The viewing figures for *Pot Black* were still climbing, and when Steve turned professional in 1978, he made his debut. In a short space of time, his name wasn't celebrated only in snooker halls across the country, but in households, too. As for my dad, he found himself sitting on a portfolio of snooker halls that had amassed significant value. When the investment company sold their share, Dad made his first million. He didn't sit back, however. If anything, he got more into the business of the sport.

Steve was making a serious name for himself, with my dad getting him into all the big tournaments such as the World Championships. Dad's an energetic and likeable man, and other players could see what he was doing with Steve's career. They wanted a piece of the action, too, as well as the flash suits and the media, and before long he was representing some of the best players in the world. From the late, great Willie Thorne to Jimmy White, Cliff Thorburn, Terry Griffiths, Ronnie O'Sullivan and Dennis Taylor, they all came under Dad's wing, and the company he founded to manage them, which was named after his snooker hall in Romford: Matchroom.

By the time I was born, Barry Hearn was on his way to becoming a household name. Snooker was the rock and roll sport of the time. Not only was Dad in the right place, he made the most of it. Looking back, I can understand why he wasn't around that much, but he certainly looked after his family. We moved from Ongar to Brentwood, which two decades later would turn into the company headquarters. They were happy days, and Dad's work was dazzling to me.

I don't think he understood or cared too much about plotting or planning a long-term business back then. He was riding the wave, and slowly taking over the sport, and he got himself into a position where he was controlling the sport. It made him untouchable, with incredible rewards for the deals he was doing. Given this was the eighties, he'd go out and buy Ferraris with Steve, or the white Merc with the 147 number plate, so everyone knew who was behind the wheel. Matchroom even had a limo that took the players on tour around the country, living on the road from one tournament to the next. The driver would sometimes pick me up from school in it – I felt the nuts, but looking back it makes me cringe.

Then snooker took off around the globe, especially in the Far East, and Dad and the Matchroom team would fly out to China and the rest of South East Asia. There would be thousands of people waiting to greet them at the airport. Steve was treated like a god out there, and in all the pictures of him, I'd see my dad in his flash silver suit looking as if he was having the time of his life. You have to understand that this was a kid from Dagenham who'd made more than good, and you can see it in his grin. Happy days.

Back home, I spent a lot of time with my mum, my sister

and my grandparents. We were a close, solid family, who happened to be living an increasingly good life, thanks to Dad and the money he was bringing back. The appetite for snooker was huge, and he was happy to feed it with all kinds of offshoot projects. By his own admission, he didn't always know what he was doing, but it worked. Mostly by accident but sometimes design, he began to forge a brand for the business. From a range of aftershaves to timeshare apartments in Spain called the Matchroom Country Club, my dad kept on cresting that wave.

A few years after we moved to Brentwood, he got his players together and they called themselves the Matchroom Mob, and recorded a song with Chas and Dave. 'Snooker Loopy' went to number six in the UK charts. They recorded a video for it too, which Dad was in, and that made him as familiar to the public as his players.

Barry Hearn was a pioneer in many ways, but the fundamentals of good business that he would go on to teach me weren't always evident in his work back then. His approach was sometimes reckless and always fun – a kind of nothing-to-lose attitude – and some of the moves he made take my breath away now.

There were other times, however, when he made decisions that revealed his basic values to me. Dad once staged a televised tournament featuring all his players, and secured prize-money sponsorship for £600,000. It went on for two weeks and proved a massive hit, but behind the scenes, the company that had promised the sponsorship went bust. With the prize-money pot gone, my dad paid out from his own pocket. He nearly went bankrupt himself in the process, but as far as he was concerned, it was the only option available to him. It's what he's like, an honourable man. He talked about it over dinner with my mum, and I sat there listening.

'Why didn't you just tell the players the sponsors had gone under?' Mum asked, because Dad's decision to pay out had put Matchroom into considerable debt. 'They'd understand.'

'Maybe I could have done,' he said, 'but I'd given my word they would be paid.'

I played no part in these conversations, of course, but in my young mind I registered them. As I came to understand what made my dad tick, I took on board the importance of doing what's right, even when everything else is going wrong. Without doubt those early years were a learning experience for him, and in some ways an education for me.

It also continued after we'd left the table. Dad would go to his study to make work calls, having promised me that once he'd finished, we could play a sport of my choosing before bed. I'd wait around outside his office, hoping he'd get off the phone. Like any kid, however, I got restless. Through the door, I could hear him talking, laughing and arguing.

Towards the late eighties he'd got into boxing as well, which made him even busier. All I wanted him to do was finish whatever business was taking up his time, so we could play some table tennis before Mum called for me and I had to go to bed. In the end, thinking perhaps he'd forgotten all about me, I'd slip into his office. With the phone to his ear, my dad would respond by holding me at arm's length. I'd get the message that I was bothering him, but not want to back out. So, I'd lie on the carpet beside his chair, effectively under his radar. Usually I had a cricket ball with me. On my back, facing the ceiling, I'd toss it into the air and catch it repeatedly.

I never set out to listen in to those calls, but subconsciously I was registering how my dad conducted business. I took in every twist and turn of a negotiation, or change in tone or emotion if he was dealing with a rival promoter. The details went over my head, but the outcome was always the same. A deal was there for the making, no matter what it took. I could be there on the floor for ten minutes or an hour. It didn't matter to me. I knew that eventually Dad would put down that phone, shoot me a grin, and I would have him all to myself across the table-tennis net. Like the cricket, he played with absolute concentration and conviction, and in the same way I learned to become a match for him. That was how life was for me, growing up at home.

At school it was a different story.

I went to Brentwood School. It's fee-paying, with a mixture of posh kids and those whose parents had made their money and moved out of East London. It's housed mostly in a grand old building and boasts a wide range of former pupils who have made a name for themselves, such as Frank Lampard, Noel Edmonds, Keith Allen and Griff Rhys Jones. There, everyone knew me by my father. I was never Eddie Hearn, always Barry Hearn's son, but that was fine then, because how many people have a famous dad? I realised it brought me attention and some status, and I milked it.

I'll be frank, I was a right prat at school – horrible. A proper Flash Harry in a posh boy's uniform. Sometimes Dad would pick me up in Matchroom's white stretch limo, and I loved it if everyone was looking. In those days, you didn't hire out those vehicles for hen nights. They were the business! Success on four wheels. It's cringe now, of course, but back then I'd let a couple of my mates pile in the back with me, music on, windows down as my dad pulled away, and I'd revel in the attention. I was truly obnoxious as a kid, but that was the world I lived in.

In some ways, Dad's growing interests in boxing made things even worse. In 1987, he put on Frank Bruno versus Joe Bugner at White Hart Lane. With fighters on his books such as Nigel Benn, Chris Eubank, and Naseem Hamed, I went from being the flash kid with a famous dad to the flash kid who thought he could fight.

Truth be told, I was a bit soft when push came to shove. I happened to be taller than most, and used my height and size to my advantage. Thanks to my old man, I got to hang around with the boxers we idolised, and often flew around the world to watch them fight. It meant I could swagger into class on a Monday, having spent the weekend in New York with Lennox Lewis, or Hong Kong with Herbie Hide. It was such an easy way to impress people, and obviously totally shallow, but it worked. I really thought I was the nuts! In fact, I was a complete knob.

As honesty is the only way forward in life and business, I have to admit that in my time at Brentwood I probably wasn't the nicest kid. I'm not proud to admit it, but it's true. If anything, I was simply boisterous – even so, that's no excuse. I didn't go looking for trouble, but because of my bad attitude, I'd find it. What was behind it? I guess insecurity played a big part, and that has only left me in the last ten years or so, as I've started to make my own mark. As a kid living in my dad's shadow, however, I found it hard to be myself. I've always been good at projecting confidence, even though I didn't have it at school, and sometimes that played out in unnecessary ways.

Naturally, I wish I could go back and have a word with that kid now. At the time, my dad did that instead. I'd come home from school and brag about a fight I'd had in the playground. Next thing, he'd have me up against the wall, growling,

'Think you're tough now, eh?' That kind of reaction from my old man really hit home. All I can say is that everything we experience when growing up shapes us for the better once we're mature enough to process it. I couldn't help the fact that my dad hung out with boxers we considered to be gods. That's just how it was.

As a schoolboy, living this unusual life at home, my problem with authority took centre stage. There I was, the son of an untouchable as it seemed to me, and I didn't react well to being put in my place by anyone other than him.

A teacher would yell at me, 'Hearn! That's it, you're staying behind after school!' In response, I'd screw up my face, thinking, *Who are you? I know Chris Eubank!*

It's kind of funny now, but my attitude was *terrible*. I feel so sorry for my mum. She's bright and smart, and had high hopes that I'd shine academically. All she wanted was for me to be a good student like my older sister, who aced school with top grades. Instead, she got lumbered with this son who would deliberately provoke a teacher on his way out of detention and then promptly earn another.

Even when I was behaving myself, my attention span was lousy. I was one of those pupils who didn't try unless I understood something immediately, or you could find a way to motivate me. Some teachers had my measure. They recognised that if they found a way in with me, I could be motivated, but it was a rare thing. As a result, I was a bang average student, who tended to fold his arms and stare out of the window.

When I was fourteen, I began to think perhaps I had a chance in the ring. I was a big lad, loved the sport, and liked to spar whenever I had a chance. I had a couple of fights as an amateur, under the name Eddie Hills, because my dad thought my surname would make me a target. At my first fight, I didn't even know he'd switched my name until I was introduced in the blue corner. There I was, giving it the big one, when I hear this other name being called out and suddenly I'm wondering if there's been a mix-up with the cards. I did win all my fights, even though I was bang average.

My dad always promised me that at eighteen, he would get me in the ring and teach me a lesson. Two years earlier than expected, as I continued to grow, he felt it was time.

'Come on, son. Let's do this.'

When Dad invited me to take him on, I knew he wouldn't pull his punches. Having grown up facing him at all sports, I had no doubt he'd try to lay me out, and so I took it really seriously. There aren't many fathers and sons who have gone toe to toe in the boxing ring. Yes, it felt weird as we danced around each other with our gloves raised, but in a way I expected nothing less from him.

As soon as the bell went, Dad started to let his hands go and he put it on me with gritted teeth. He hit me with a big right hand down the pipe. Then I came back at him in the second round and dropped him twice with body shots. He even gave interviews about it at the time – it shows how proud he was, to boast about getting knocked out by a 16-year-old. If anything, he savoured his defeat more than I did the victory.

'I just wanted to make sure what you were made of,' he told me, and to this day I look back at that episode as one of the moments I showed him.

My career as a boxer ended there, because I was involved in so many other sports at school and I was also useless. That was my saving grace, where I showed true grit and drive. I was built for rugby, which I really enjoyed, and though I was rubbish at football, that didn't matter to me. I loved to play, but if there was one thing I loved even more, it was winning. I have my dad to thank for that, of course. He wasn't like most parents, who would stress the importance of taking part. That didn't matter to him. He wanted me to be on the side that *smashed* the opposition, and if that didn't happen, it was a failure.

Fortunately, when it came to cricket, I had something to offer. As Dad had given me no quarter from the moment I picked up a bat, I was decent on the pitch. I found that I was good enough to be selected to play for Essex from the Under-13s on up for several years, and even went on international tours.

For me, school was a chance for me to make my name with a ball or a bat. That was where I made my contribution. So, at sixteen, when I picked up my envelope on GCSE results day to find I'd missed out on the grades I needed to pass for sixth form, I figured my track record in sport would see me through. That's how it worked at the school. It was really nothing to worry about, I figured.

'I know Eddie didn't quite make it over the line,' my dad said in the school meeting convened to hear his case, 'but he's in the first team for cricket, he's in the football team and will develop into a real asset for the school.'

I've no doubt my dad made a strong case for them to take me on, but this was one deal he failed to make. The school had made up their mind about me, and their decision was final. It felt like the end of the world when I learned the outcome. I was genuinely shocked and embarrassed, but the fact was that my attitude and behaviour over the years had tested staff to breaking point.

'Nah,' they said, pretty much. 'We're not letting your son into sixth form.'

'Oh, come on,' my dad reasoned. 'Don't be daft!'

'I'm sorry, Mr Hearn. That's it for Eddie at Brentwood.'

ROUND 1 – KEY TAKEAWAYS

- If you want to see results, face them head on and don't back down.

- The only thing stopping your progress and development is yourself.

- A deal is always there in the making, no matter what it takes.

- You are never too busy, it's simply a matter of priorities.

- Honesty is the only way forward in life and business.

- If it's important to you, you will find a way. If not, you will find an excuse.

Round 2

TOUGH SELL

'So what?' I said, when Dad came home to break the news about the school's decision. 'I'll just get a job.'

It was all a front, of course, and I certainly wasn't ready to enter the real world. I couldn't believe they'd refused to have me back, and both Mum and Dad were having none of my bravado. They would have to find a school prepared to take me, they said, which turned out to be easier said than done.

With my average grades, the only place we could find was Havering Sixth Form College in Romford. This was a far cry from my last school. There was no uniform or anything like that. It was full of kids, mainly from East London, who didn't know what they wanted to do with their lives. Mum was reluctant to send me, but one thing I'd become good at was being thrown in at the deep end.

Travelling around the world with Dad, I was used to walking into a rowdy, heated or even hostile environment and feeling that I'd be looked after. Once we went to Germany to watch one of Dad's boxers fight for the European title. A riot broke out in the crowd, but it never seemed liked a big deal.

It helped that I was often with boxers who seemed happy to have me around. In truth, they probably thought they had

27

to be nice to me as I was Barry Hearn's son, but I looked on them as my best mates. It meant I could walk into a Bethnal Green boxing gym and feel that I belonged. Sometimes I'd tag along with them to watch Spurs play from the stands. I was young, but I never worried if things got rough. So, I didn't share my mum's anxiety about something as simple as a sixth form college.

On my first day, Mum dropped me off in the car. She pulled up at the steps, said goodbye, and watched me heading for the entrance. Then, so she tells me, she burst into tears. She sat there and wept. As a parent, I suppose it's one of those defining moments. For me, I knew what I had to do to establish my place.

So, I found my class, sat down and listened to the introductory talk. I started talking to a few people at morning break, and by lunchtime everyone had heard of me. I'd basically spent my time telling people I was Barry Hearn's son. Next thing I knew, I'd got all these people gravitating towards me. It meant when I got home after my first day and found my mum with puffy eyes, I couldn't understand her concerns.

For my A levels, I chose to study Business Studies, PE, and Media Studies. Desperate for me not to screw up again, Dad decided I needed some motivation to knuckle down.

'Here's what I'm going to do, son,' he told me. 'For every pass you get, I'm going to give you a grand.'

'You're on,' I said. 'But what if I get an A?'

Dad just laughed.

'Don't be daft. That's never going to happen.'

'But what if I do,' I persisted, and hassled him for an answer.

'Alright,' he said, giving in finally. 'Get an A, I'll give you *ten* grand.'

After everything that had happened at Brentwood, and with

a chance to make some decent money at the end of it, I was determined to get my head down at college. I was also keen to get into some teams and keep up the side of school that I'd loved.

'What's the sports situation?' I asked a teacher at college in that first week.

The teacher looked at me.

'We don't really do sport here,' he told me. 'Sorry.'

I couldn't believe what I was hearing. Apparently there was a casual football club after lessons on a Thursday, but it had barely enough players for a team and no hope of a proper match. It was rubbish and I was gutted. No sport seemed unthinkable! Even so, I wasn't going to let that derail me in the first week. My first lesson was Business Studies. There were about eighteen of us in the room. The next session, half the seats were empty. On my way in the next time, I saw a couple of students I'd been hanging out with. They were on their way into town, and asked if I wanted to join them.

'But we've got Business Studies,' I reminded them.

'Yeah, fuck that,' one said and, sure enough, within a short while I was skipping the session to hang with them outside a newsagents in Romford.

I didn't stop going to college altogether. Once I showed up, along with a handful of students, and wondered if there would come a time when the teacher faced a completely empty class.

'There's not many people here, is there?' I said to him at the end of that lesson. 'What happens if you don't show up?'

I had expected him to say that eventually parents would be called in, or something like that. Instead, he shrugged and shook his head.

'There's nothing I can do about it, is there?'

'Yeah, but are you allowed to stay on?' I asked.

The teacher had been in a hurry to pack up his stuff and head out. He paused to consider me for a moment, and then set his papers back on the desk.

'Eddie, it's up to you,' he said. 'This isn't school. If you want to learn, it's all here. If you don't, well, you're probably going to come out of here with no qualifications and no hope of finding a job. But nobody is going to make that decision for you. It's your responsibility now.'

His advice hit me hard. It was the first time I had no authority to fight against and perhaps the moment when everything clicked, and I realised that the future was in my hands alone. Before this, my experience at school was mostly about getting yelled at and then yelling back twice as loud. I still had a problem with authority, but now I realised they had no problem with me. If I wanted to squander this opportunity, they would simply sit back and watch. My future was on me.

Having gone through school with no fear of detention or consequences, all of a sudden I faced the possibility of fucking up my life. Frankly, that was a frightening thought, and the first time I'd ever experienced such a thing. It was also what I needed. To get on in life, we need to be a little bit fearful of what's ahead. It keeps us focused, on our toes and prepared. Just then, in the course of a brief exchange with my teacher, I understood that I had one last chance at saving this.

At Brentwood, I didn't give a fuck. I could find myself marched in front of the head or face a string of detentions. My attitude was 'so what?' Now, with all threat of punishment removed, I felt weirdly motivated to prove to myself that I could do the work. So, rather than messing around in town, I started attending all my lectures. At break time, with nobody around, I'd go to the library. Sometimes I'd work through lunch, and then go down to the gym in Romford and hang out with the fighters.

I didn't really have friends at college, but I was close to those guys. They'd take me with them to Pizza Hut, where I'd take on everything you can eat for £3.99! I was a bit chubby in those days, so those meals didn't help, but it was fun. I had a decent balance to my life, and was getting the work done.

My mum was certainly relieved to see me focused at last. We've always been a tight, protective family. Like any parent, she wanted the best for me. As a teenager, of course, I also wanted some independence, and so too did my sister, Katie. That was fine, but sometimes Mum worried about us and that's when she dispatched Dad to check we were safe and sound.

When Katie went to university down in Bournemouth, she drove herself there in her blue Fiesta.

'Call us when you get there,' Mum said. 'Just to let us know you're alright.'

We didn't have mobile phones in those days. I guess Katie went down, moved in, met up with her new housemates and went for a drink. Back home, Mum was beside herself. She told Dad to call the police, who went round and knocked on her door. My poor sister was only guilty of going out and having a good time, but our parents meant well.

I experienced their protective side one weekend when I went clubbing with friends. We used to go to this place in Romford called Hollywoods. I was only about sixteen. Too young to drive, but with fake ID in my pocket to get in, I'd catch the train from Brentwood and meet my mates outside. I'd arranged to be there for eight o'clock, only to find the trains were delayed when I got to the station – all I could do was stand around and wait. Meanwhile my friends in Romford were wondering where I was. One of them called the house and spoke to my mum, who immediately assumed the worst.

A little later than planned that evening, but still in good time, I found my mates in the queue and we waited to be let in. Hollywoods was massively popular back then. The queue snaked around the building, full of people who looked a lot cooler and older than me. All I wanted to do was blend in. So, there I was with my friends, ID in hand as we tested each other on our fake dates of birth, and suddenly I heard the noise of a familiar engine. As a kid, back home, I used to be so excited to hear my old man's white Merc approaching. This time, as a teenager, when I saw it pulling up across the road, I cringed so hard the wax in my barnet nearly melted.

I thought the window might come down, but instead the door opened, and my dad stepped out. It took me a moment to register that he was wearing his slippers. He stood there squinting, as he trained his gaze up and down the queue.

'Oi, Eddie,' said one of my mates, who probably wondered why I was staring so hard at my shoes. 'Isn't that Bazza?'

I had two choices. I could keep my head down and hope he didn't see me, but I knew he wouldn't give up because he'd have to report back to mum. So, I took the only choice available to me, dying on the inside as I stepped out of the queue and scuttled towards the man who had everyone's attention.

'Alright, son?' he asked on seeing me.

'Dad, fuck off!' I hissed under my breath.

'Your mum was worried,' he said, and gave me the thumbs up as he backed towards the Merc. 'We just wanted to check you're alright!'

My dad was the last person I wanted to see at that moment, but his heart was in the right place. It always has been, and my sister would agree. Knowing my family would be there for me meant I could be bold as I found my wings. In terms of building mindset, it was a positive force. I just wish my old man had got dressed properly before he drove into Romford that night.

With college going well, despite the lack of sport, I realised I could enjoy myself a little more if I earned some cash. Despite my upbringing, I was never spoiled. One of the fundamental lessons in life that Dad taught me was the value of money. If I wanted to earn some for myself when I was younger, then I'd have to shine his shoes. He'd pay me 50 pence a pair and I'd work my way through eight of them. Not only that, the shoes weren't ready until I could see my reflection in them, because he'd expect me to do the job well. It's a valuable lesson, and it meant I grew up happy to put in the graft.

Dad also encouraged me to sell programmes at his boxing shows, which introduced me to the concept of the tough sell. Not every punter wants to part with a few quid they've got earmarked for a pint, as I learned from experience. I was no more than thirteen or fourteen years old, but I had to find my voice amid adults and attempt to strike up a conversation. I may have played on the fact that I was still a kid to my advantage, but as Dad had put me on a commission, I also learned to banter a little bit and to pull on heartstrings.

Around the same time, I showed more initiative when it came to striking a deal for myself. Having made it to county level in cricket, playing for the Essex under-16 side, I decided that I should follow my old man's example and seek some sponsorship. To be fair, he encouraged me to go for it. His view was that if I wanted stuff, then nobody was going to offer it to me – I'd have to ask.

So, I started calling up companies from the phone book saying, 'I represent Essex and if you can give me some free gear,

I'll wear it exclusively.' If that didn't work, I'd say I was Barry Hearn's son. I imagine most people put their hand over the mouthpiece of the phone and laughed. I did get one positive response, though, from a cricket bat manufacturer run by the ex-cricketer Duncan Fearnley. The company offered me a bat, a pair of gloves and pads, probably to get rid of me. I went up to the factory to collect the gear myself, though I had to pay for the bag to bring it all home.

Naturally, I thought I had arrived. I even called the *Brentwood Gazette* and they took my picture to go with the story. I'm not sure I could face looking at it now, but I definitely wasn't shy about putting myself out there to get ahead.

A few years later, Dad made the purchase of a lifetime by saving Leyton Orient Football Club from a rough financial patch. As the new owner, he gave me the chance to earn some holiday money by selling advertising space in the season programme. It was hardly the opportunity of a lifetime for hard-pressed local businesses, but I wanted the cash. It could be difficult at times, and the deals were few and far between, but I badly wanted to prove to my dad that I could nail it. I found I even enjoyed rising to the challenge in possibly the toughest task of all – telesales.

After my A level studies, I set out to make some decent money. If I wanted stuff, or cash in my pocket for a night out, I had to earn it. Having cut my teeth with the boxing and football programmes, I looked in the local paper for part-time telesales in the Romford area. When I found vacancies at a company called Weatherseal, asking for no prior experience, I figured I'd send in my application. They called me in for an interview.

I expected to find a busy office, but this was essentially a telesales sausage factory. There were different rooms depending on the nature of the call, whether it was speculative or follow-ups, and rooms for the sales team who actually went out to see the customers. The job on offer, for several hours each week, was cold calling. All I had to do was ring Mr Jones out of the blue, persuade him to express an interest in a consultation, and bosh! I'd pass that lead through to the next department, take the commission, and get on with finding the next lead.

I must have made all the right noises, and for once I didn't mention my dad, because I got the job. On my first shift, after college ended one afternoon, they put me in a room crammed with desks and people who looked as if they hadn't breathed fresh air in quite a while. Most of them had cans of Coke on the go, massive bags of crisps, or cigarettes in an ashtray. All of them were on the phones, and each had a copy of the telephone directory at their disposal. This contained the names, addresses and phone numbers for everyone in the Romford area.

'There you go,' said my supervisor, who showed me to my desk. She tapped the phone book in front of me. 'Start with M.'

As I picked up the phone, I noticed a whiteboard at the front of the room. This showed the hourly rates I could earn, depending on my success, and was marked up with who was on what. The basic rate for each session was three pounds an hour. You'd get a fiver for a lead and your rate would also go up by a quid an hour. For every lead after that, your reward and the hourly rate escalated by another pound. Looking at the scrawl on the whiteboard, before I'd made a single call, this looked mega. Easy money!

To make it even more straightforward, they provided me with a checklist of common responses from the people whose lives I was about to interrupt so I could sell them something they didn't realise they needed. From *just got new windows* to *need to speak to my husband* and everything in between, my crib sheet covered everything. I didn't even have to think. At least that's what I thought until I made my first call. I got as far as stating my name, but didn't finish saying what company I represented before the line went dead. The same thing happened with the next name in the phone book, and the one after that. After a few attempts, the girl at the desk next to me got my attention.

'That's all you're going to get,' she said casually. 'Rejections.'

Her prediction proved right on the first shift, but I didn't leave feeling defeated. I went home and researched all the windows I could offer and the options available. I also rehearsed my responses to customers, if I ever got further than introducing myself.

It took some time before I got a result, but when I did, I felt as if I had gone into battle and come out victorious. It wasn't even a guarantee that I'd sold any windows. Just a weary acceptance that a visit from one of our reps wouldn't hurt. I had earned it. In a way, the extra money didn't matter for that first sale. It was all about persistence, learning to think on my feet and not giving up.

Like all the leads that followed, that first one didn't come easy.

'Hi, this is Eddie from Weathers—'

Cut off before I could I finish, because quite clearly I was trying to sell something, I tried a second time.

'Hi, this is Ed—'

As soon as the line went dead, I hit redial.

'Hi, this—'

Undeterred, I called a fourth time. On this occasion, the poor guy I was hassling got in first.

'*What do you want?*' he bellowed. 'Stop bothering me!'

I took a breath. We had a connection.

'I don't know if you're having a bad day, sir, but this is Eddie from Weatherseal and I'd be happy to talk about it.'

'What?'

'Well, I'm having a bad day, too. I'm hoping to chat to you about windows to brighten things up, because we have an unbelievable deal on right now. It's for a limited period, but I don't want you to miss out . . .'

I could've abandoned that lead when he cut the line the first time. Instead, I sensed that if I could start a conversation I could get somewhere, and I did. I had no idea if the guy bought new windows or not. It didn't matter to me. I had that coveted piece of paper I could take next door, to confirm he'd accept a home visit, which meant chalking up an increase in the money I'd be taking home. This was cash that had nothing to do with my dad and I had earned by my own merit. It was a buzz, almost addictive, and although I'd have to work through a soul-destroying number of calls before I got somewhere, I persisted.

Whatever the objection, I was ready with a way around it.

'We've just got new windows, Eddie. But thanks very much.'

'May I ask what material the windows are made from, sir?'

'Wood.'

'Oh.'

Masterfully, I sucked the air between my teeth.

'What? Is there a problem with wood?'

'It's just all the research suggests wood erodes much faster than other materials. You could replace them now with the latest UPVC, at an incredible discount, and save yourself money in the long run.'

'Son, I've fucking told you, we've just got new windows.'

'Alright, sir. All I'm suggesting is a free consultation with one of our representatives. We can even check the job done on your existing windows. That's five minutes of your day for a lifetime's peace of mind.'

Sometimes, if all the stars aligned, a call like this would end with a sigh.

'Go on, then. If it gets you off my back.'

Within a month or so in the job, I was nailing it. Three or four times a shift, I'd drop a piece of paper on a rep's table next door and head straight back into battle. After a while, my supervisor called me in for a chat. It turned out the conversion rates from my leads to sales weren't that great. We both knew what this meant, and it was supposed to serve as a warning. In reality, I had reached the point where I was pressing reluctant customers to do me a favour and agree to a rep's visit. I knew they had no intention of buying new windows. In agreeing to leave them alone, I'd pretty much recruited them into my own blag.

There wasn't much the company could do to change that, I figured, so I carried on chasing those leads like my life depended on it. Then, after each shift as this driven telesales warrior, I'd leave the building and return to life as Eddie the sixth former. I might hang out at the gym for a bit with the boxers and then wait for my dad to give me a lift home.

After two years at Havering Sixth Form College, having learned to get my head down, I came out with a C in Business Studies, a C in PE, and that all-important A in Media Studies. Just seeing that result was a sweet moment, and I called my dad to share the news.

'I did it!' I cried. 'I got an A grade! That's ten grand, Dad. Just like we agreed, right? *Ten grand!*'

'You didn't,' was his first response, uttered in disbelief and pride. 'In what?'

'Media Studies.'

'Oh, fuck off!' Dad said. 'That doesn't count!'

So, I got three grand. One for each A level. I should've felt a bit cheated, but to be honest, the sense of achievement it gave me more than made up for the money.

I had the grades to go to university and that would set me on my way. I thought about following my sister for a short while. She was studying Leisure Marketing, which really appealed to me. At the same time, I couldn't help thinking it would end up being a wrong move in my life. Yes, the last two years of my education were a success, but I felt that my time might be better invested in the workplace, so that I'd be further up the road in the three years it would take me to get a degree. I was torn, because I fancied the social life and the sport, but in the end I decided to pass.

The obvious move for me would've have been to work for my dad. In a sense, it was also the last thing I wanted to do. Matchroom is in my blood, of course, but I needed to prove myself first. Not only to my dad and everyone around us, but I needed to demonstrate to myself that I had what it took to make a difference. Even at school, people would say I didn't have to worry as I'd be going to work for my old man, and that had become an irritation.

I knew there would always be a door open for me at Matchroom. Everything Dad had done for me was geared towards me joining him at some point, and I wanted to work for him, but on my own terms and based on achievements I had yet to make. On top of all that, Dad's office at the time was in Romford. I was eighteen, hungry to make my mark on the world, and itching to be in London.

I loved sport, and wanted to work in that field, and so I started looking at sport agency and marketing jobs. I liked the idea of representing athletes. It was one part of my dad's job that I'd always been drawn towards, and I found it easy talking to the boxers, darts and snooker players on his books. I wrote off to about two dozen sports management and event companies. About half of them replied to say they had nothing, and a couple asked me in for a meeting.

I was excited about the invitation from IMG, which is a global sports and talent management business. It was over in Mortlake, which took me about two hours to reach by bus, train, tube and on foot, and might as well have been on the other side of the world. I walked into the office, dressed up and hoping to impress. The guy came down to meet me, shook my hand and looked at me searchingly.

'Can I just ask,' he said. 'Are you Barry Hearn's son?'

My heart sank a bit, because I wanted to strike out on my own. They ended up offering me an internship, which was really work experience for no salary that only rich kids like me could afford to do. I didn't want to fall into that, and so I politely declined.

Next I went to see another company who had asked me in. They were called BDS Sponsorship, a smaller but impressive operation in Covent Garden, which was run by a guy called Richard Busby.

'Are you Barry Hearn's son?' he asked, before we'd even sat down for a chat. 'What are you doing looking for a job with us?'

Patiently, I explained why I didn't want to work for my dad. I was fresh from cutting my teeth in double-glazing telesales, I told him, and wanted to combine sales with sport. To my surprise, this sales pitch for myself worked. Busby took me on as a Sponsorship Executive, a title I think he made up on the spot, and I practically strutted out of that building. I was on a salary of twelve thousand a year, which made me feel like a million dollars. I even went out and got my own business cards printed.

In a flattering light, my role as Sponsorship Executive involved consulting companies who wanted to get into backing sports or events. Cadbury had started sponsoring the Premiership, for example, and they were a client. Not that I had anything to do with that. In reality most of my time was spent compiling a database, and involved calling companies to ask for the contact details for their marketing people. I was sharing an office with Busby, who also spent a lot of time on his phone. Every now and then he'd reach for his empty coffee cup, deep in conversation down the line with someone, and stretch out his arm in my direction. I would take that as my cue to break off my own work and make him a fresh brew.

I had no reason to complain about the work. It was hard and repetitive, but I wasn't shy of doing the graft. Even making the coffee was part of my job, and I did it to the best of my abilities. I was young, earning decent money, and able to let off steam with my mates in town every Friday night. It meant I'd come in on a Monday feeling refreshed and good to go again. After a while, I suppose my personality on the phone started to come through. I was confident, bold and engaging, and Busby began to pay attention. He had plans to set up a sponsorship conference, and asked me to get involved.

With a decent database in place, I started going through my contacts, selling packages to marketing directors. The approach I took wasn't far off what I was doing at Weatherseal, and frankly I started smashing it. Back then, the concept of sponsoring events was cool and kind of groundbreaking, so this time

I had something to sell that sounded decent. A package for the event cost just under five hundred quid, and I was selling ten a day. I felt as if I'd come into my own, and each win boosted my confidence to hunt down another.

Eventually, we got six hundred delegates in the bag. The event turned out to be quite a success, and Busby rewarded me for my efforts by asking me to head up a whole sponsorship sales department. I wasn't dealing with the big league stuff, like a deal that BDS had set up for BT to sponsor Hampden Park stadium in Glasgow. That was overseen by the senior sales staff. My role was to put together the bread-and-butter deals that helped pay the rent on our new HQ in Islington. I even had my own office there in an annexe from the main building. It meant if the phone rang, as it did one day six months into the move, nobody could hear me.

'Eddie Hearn. BDS. How can I help?'

'Hi there,' the caller said, and introduced herself as representing a recruitment agency. 'I wonder if you could tell me who is in charge of sales?'

I glanced around to double check there was nobody within earshot from the main department.

'That'll be me,' I confirmed quietly.

From there the caller explained that she was inviting a selection of sales directors to apply for a position with London Events Agency. They were a big deal at the time, representing decent names in sport and staging reputable global events.

'Would you be interested in the post?' the caller asked me.

I was nineteen years old, and by then I was earning eighteen thousand pounds a year. That was a lot of money for a kid my age.

'I am interested,' I said, hoping to sound casual. 'Can I ask about the salary?'

'It's in the region of thirty-three thousand,' said the caller. 'With bonuses.'

A moment passed before I realised I should say something.

'Yeah, that's similar to my package now,' I confirmed, as convincingly as I could, and within minutes I had secured an interview when I least expected it.

My elation didn't last long. By the end of that day, reality set in. I had bluffed my way into an interview for a job that was way above my pay grade. I figured I had two options. Either I failed to show up, which wasn't in my nature, or I gave it my best shot.

On the day, I arrived for the interview in my best suit, hoping nobody would cotton on that I was shitting myself. Then I set about covering for myself with a masterclass in bullshit. The Hampden Park deal? Yes, I was on the team for that. You know Cadbury? I'm their go-to consultant with the Premiership. It was all over in a blaze of bollocks, and I left thinking I'd never see those people again.

A few days later, I was called back for a second interview.

At this stage, I told my dad what was going on. I was fired up at the prospect of seeing my salary sky-rocket, but he was mostly focused on the fact that I had blagged my way this far.

'Just be careful, son,' he said. 'Don't get ahead of yourself.'

With this in mind, I went into that interview determined to play it straight, and ended up inflating my achievements all over again. I was selling myself, of course; pursuing a deal like I had on the phones at Weatherseal. When I'd finished painting myself as the saviour of the global sponsorship industry, one of the guys on the panel levelled with me.

'Listen, Eddie, we really like you. You've got confidence, you think on your feet and show great initiative, but here's the thing. You're nineteen years old, and everyone else we've short-listed has been in the game for at least ten to fifteen years. Can you see the concerns we might have?'

In my mind, as he set out his case, I might as well have been listening to a homeowner explain why this wasn't the time for him to invest in double glazing. On finishing, he'd barely drawn breath before I set out to salvage the deal.

'I see your point,' I agreed, 'but I've been in this business all my life. I've been nurtured to this moment, and what you'll get from me is the energy, the passion and the sheer determination. I don't have kids or a wife or any of the restrictions. That means I can give you a hundred and twenty per cent and be flat out every single day. I promise you,' I concluded, 'there will be nobody hungrier than me.'

In the moment that followed, the panel looked at me in stunned silence. When they offered me the job, calling me with the good news a day later, I had to hold back my excitement at the news.

'So, that will be with the package proposed?' I asked solemnly, having fist-pumped the air in my office.

'Eddie, we feel like thirty-three thousand is rather a lot for someone your age. Will you accept thirty thousand?'

This was still twelve thousand more than I was on.

'Let me have a think about that,' I said, urging myself not to bite his hand off, and promptly called my dad, who refused to believe me. I was pumped and wanted to share the news with him.

'Prove yourself to them,' he suggested. 'Show them what you're worth.'

So, I went back and agreed the terms. I told them I didn't want to quibble about money. I planned to demonstrate they had made a solid investment that would guarantee them a return, and a chance to review the package in due course. Yes, it was all front, but I really did want to prove them right.

The new offices were based in Covent Garden. The commute took me almost two hours, but I arrived earlier for work than most and was one of the last to leave at the end of each day. I had seized an opportunity that arguably wasn't mine, and then talked myself into believing they had picked the right guy for the job. Within the first few weeks, through hard work and a little bit of luck, I landed a nice little sponsorship deal for Ian Botham with a cider manufacturer. It didn't make anyone rich, but it bought me a lot of confidence.

I can't say that blagging guarantees success in sales, but it does play a part in the strategy. I knew I was good at it, but after two years I began to feel that I was calling on experience, rather than chancing my arm. In turn, that gave me the confidence to be ambitious. Early in my time there, Dad was staging a Naseem Hamed fight and so I approached him as anyone else would about bringing in a sponsor. Like our own bout in the ring, I think he wanted to see what I could do. As a result, I brought in a six-figure Budweiser contract. Dad was happy and my employees were fucking blown away. It was a big step up and another learning experience, but the success spurred me on.

Once I got over the sense that I had lucked my way into the job, and began to prove my worth to myself and my employers, I started representing golfers. This involved signing them up to take part in the European Tour and managing the sponsorship deals this attracted. I worked in this field for about twelve months and, to be honest, I got a bit carried away with myself.

I was only in my early twenties, and hadn't quite shaken off the issue with authority that first took hold at school. I was out there in the sponsorship world, working my nuts off to pull in lucrative deals, and the directors were asking me for progress reports. This needled me, because they had only to look at the figures to see that I was knocking it out of the park. Why did they need a record of how I got there? As a result, I would drag my heels about delivering the summaries. It annoyed them as much as it irritated me, and though it wasn't a major problem, it encouraged me to think it was time to move on.

Having made my mark working for others, I figured it was time I stepped out on my own.

ROUND 2 – KEY TAKEAWAYS

- Nobody is going to make a decision for you; it's yours alone. The future is in your hands and you have the possibility to shape it as you wish.

- Don't confuse being relentless with being fearless. You need to be a little fearful of what's ahead. It keeps you on your toes, focused and prepared, and can also help you manage expectations.

- Behind every success is a ton of failure. Don't think that people haven't shared that same disappointment and rejection on the way to the top.

- Success is addictive, but remember there are no short-cuts on any road worth travelling.

Round 3

ALL IN

It feels good to be ambitious. With a plan, it brings confidence and focus, and I was aiming high. I'd spent a year working hard to promote golfers for LEA. Now I set my sights on setting up my own company. It seemed like a limitless opportunity. All I needed was the platform to launch.

I could've gone to my dad, of course, and pitched him with a view to expanding Matchroom into the golf market, but I still didn't feel ready to join the family business outright. I was going places with my career, and I'd achieved it on my own terms. At the same time, I talked to Dad about my plans as they shaped up, and he put forward a suggestion that I couldn't refuse.

'I represent some golfers who are ready to come on board if you'll back me,' I said in a meeting with two big players in the sports management world, who I hoped would invest a 50-percent stake in the business. 'We could bring in a sponsor to back our team of golfers and wrap it all under the Matchroom brand.'

I knew it was a good offer, and when the pair went for it, so Matchroom Golf came into existence. With no need to invest money, there was very little risk to my dad – and this was my chance to start my transition without a leg up. He'd reached a point in life where the business was on a solid footing. He'd diversified into other sports such as darts and fishing, and had left behind the tendency to throw himself into ventures that in hindsight could be seen as risky.

My proposal was a good one; though it wasn't going to contribute massively to the coffers compared to his main interests, golf was a good look. So, operating under the Matchroom name, with no financial liability, suited us both. It meant I could come under the family name, while still maintaining my independence. As I saw things, for the investors as much as the golfers who came with me, it was a win for us all.

The downside of my plan for global golf domination was that I spent barely a day of the next few years at home.

Golf is big business in America. A lot of the major tours take place over there. My role was to manage my clients, build their profiles and maximise their returns. In reality, that meant taking care of everything they needed to do their jobs. From booking competitions for a golfer, flights, accommodation and visas, to travelling out there with them and following them around one course after another. Should they double bogey on the eighteenth, crashing out, I'd have to deal with the media and then serve as a counsellor and psychologist.

I looked after the players' sponsorship, learned to advise them on tax planning, and made sure they could focus on the game that brought in the money. Even in those rare times when I was back in the UK, I could receive a call from a golfer at four in the morning because a flight had been cancelled, and it was on me to get him on a plane.

Sometimes I'd make a mistake and then drop everything to resolve it in order to keep the show on the road. I was once woken up in the middle of the night by one of my clients who had landed at Atlanta and found nobody there to collect him.

'I'll give the car company a nudge,' I said, knowing full well I'd clean forgotten to book it.

It was always a scramble to get over these hurdles, but it taught me to pay attention to detail, and never make the same mistake twice. The key to success is what you make of your failures. So, learning from your mistakes, whatever they might be, is an important step in your career and journey to the top. Back then, I was like a PA in many ways. It left me with weird bits of knowledge about dealing with others and how things work that I still use to this day. I might fly into America, with time ticking before I need to be at a press conference, and find myself outside the airport in the same situation as my stranded golfer. You can never underestimate what you learn along the way! Every penny of that business was on me. So east or west coast – I'd always fly economy class. At 6ft 5", a bad back after a ten hour flight always seemed like a wise investment if it meant saving a grand.

Matchroom Golf was an intense, sometimes hectic experience, but incredible grounding for learning how to deal with people, pressure and responsibility. It involved a great deal of hard work, without ever truly switching off, but there were rewards for our efforts.

I had one player, a lovely guy called John Morgan, who had just turned professional. I persuaded him to enter qualifying school for the prestigious PGA tour. It's a competitive series of stages, because everyone wants to play at the highest level, but I had faith in John. So, we flew out together to Dixon, Tennessee, hired a car and then drove around the state looking for the golf course. After he qualified at the first stage, it took us to the next stage in Orlando, Florida, where he also came out on top. Then we took the flight west to California, and there he won his PGA tour card.

The next thing I knew, I was negotiating a deal on the 18th green with Nike for half a million dollars. Immediately, John's profile increased along with his marketing potential. He used to dye his hair bright colours, which made him stand out among the other players. At one tournament, the PGA commissioner came up to me and he was clearly uncomfortable with it.

'Can I ask how long John plans to keep his hair blue?' he asked.

'Only until next month,' I said, much to his relief, though it didn't last long. 'He plans to go pink after that.'

One time John came within a whisker of winning a major PGA tournament. Nike would've renegotiated the deal in an instant had he done so, and made us millions. It was a high-stakes game in some ways; exhausting, but I loved it.

For three years, I pretty much lived on the road. From New York to Los Angeles, Atlanta, Hawaii, and then across to Europe, I basically followed the tournaments. No matter how motivated you are, however, the constant travel slowly grinds you down. I was flying economy everywhere, as I did the business accounts and knew I couldn't afford to upgrade. In fact, I wasn't able to stretch my legs in more ways than one. Matchroom Golf was profitable. We just weren't making serious money. Even so, I had learned a whole lot of invaluable lessons from the experience. I had done everything on my own initiative, and felt that I could hold my own in the world of sports management. In terms of business grounding, I was ready. I knew that a career in golf wasn't going to define me, but I knew I was growing as an operator and businessman.

It was time, at last, to join the family fold.

I was in my mid-twenties when I went to work for Matchroom. I'm sure Dad would've taken me on board after college, but I needed to earn my stripes independently if I was going to hold my head up high. Living out of a suitcase, being on call night and day, and the constant commitment to my golfers' best interests, gave me the confidence to know that when I finally joined the company, it wouldn't be by birthright, but as an asset.

During my time in the States, I'd found myself getting interested in poker. I'd watch late-night games on hotel televisions, noticed how it was picking up in popularity online, and I even played a bit whenever I got the opportunity. What drew me was the characters in a game, and that came down to the players. On screen, they'd be larger than life.

On one side of the table you'd have a guy with a beard down to his waist called Jesus. Facing him would be some maths geek just out of college, and then some old gangster in a fedora, shades and a cloud of cigarette smoke. As the game drew you in, it became compelling. I could watch for hours without realising how much time had passed. So, when I talked to my dad about packing in the golf, I figured I had found a game that I could take places.

At the time, Dad was involved in an online format called Poker Million with Ladbrokes. It meant pitching my plans to him found some early traction. He was sorry to see me leave the golf behind, simply because he loved watching our players. It was entertaining for him, and he'd get behind the golfers as if they were thoroughbreds. He still follows some of them religiously today.

'Trust me,' I said. 'Poker has potential.'

It was one thing getting my dad's buy-in. Now I had to prove myself to him, as well as everyone else at Matchroom. Dad has always been completely transparent about the way he runs his business, so all the employees know what's going on in every department. He would gather the team for monthly meetings, and then look at the status of the different sports they covered in turn. Snooker was number one at the time. It brought in the biggest return. Then there was darts and fishing, and though boxing featured, it wasn't doing much business any more. All I knew was that if I was to gain any credibility or respect, poker would have to be top of that board.

As I saw things, running the number one sport at Matchroom was the only way that I could justify my arrival. I knew it wouldn't be easy, and that I'd have to shift into a higher gear when it came to the commitment, guts and energy. I never once doubted myself, and over the course of the next two to three years, we took complete control of the televised poker market.

Yes, I was in the right place at the right time. As technology provided a platform, poker was set to ignite in this country as it had in America, but it was me who lit the touch paper and cracked *Premier League Poker* on Channel Four, *Sports Stars Challenge* for Sky, and *The Big Game* for Channel Five. It was very simple in some ways. We'd hire a studio, or even use one of the rooms at Leyton Orient FC. There, we'd set up a table, lighting and cameras, and produce content for a hungry, growing audience. In turn, we became the biggest distributor of the game worldwide. Matchroom Poker was everywhere, on screens across every country, and delivering formats to every online site across the web.

In terms of the day-to-day running of the operation, I built on the foundations I had set down with the golf. It gave me the experience I needed to deal with the problems and the personalities I'd encounter that needed overcoming in order to drive the business. Having watched the geezer with the long beard called Jesus and the old time gangster facing him across the card table from the comfort of my hotel room, I now found myself dealing with them for real. Let me tell you, these guys made boxers look like saints.

We might have a situation where I was staging a game in which every player has to buy in for fifty thousand pounds. We'd then film it and the winner would take four hundred thousand. It sounds straightforward, but getting the money out of these people before they sat down was tough. I heard every excuse and promise that the money was coming, but after my time selling windows and setting up sponsorship deals, I knew when someone was chatting shit.

'I've wired in the money and so it'll be in your account tomorrow,' a player would assure me as the cameras were ready to roll, but that's not how it worked for me. They would be convincing, and gutted when I doubted them, but there was no way that I would allow myself to risk getting burned. In sealing a deal, as I knew from experience and in listening to my dad in those early days, the only way to play things was dead straight.

'Once the money's in our possession,' I'd say, 'you can sit down to play. Until then, no deal.'

In response, it could go either way. Having failed to call my bluff, some would tell me to fuck myself and storm off. The sensible ones would miraculously conjure up the cash. Every now and then that payment would be five grand short. I'd send them away to make up the shortfall and tell them to hurry, because the filming schedule wouldn't wait for them. It was hardline but effective, and the only way to get business done. Everyone knew the rules, which were both firm and fair, and if somebody had an issue with it, they had no place at the table.

I only once got knocked by a player, for the buy-in stake. A lot of players like a drink at the table, but this guy was seriously lagging. With his eye off the game, the other players were draining him. He was determined to stay in even after his cash had run out, and so the others staked him ten thousand each.

With the cameras running, I had no choice but to throw in twenty to bring him back in, which he promised to pay me straight after the game.

Sure enough, the guy vanished, flying straight back home to America, but I didn't let it lie. I chased him for weeks, calling him dozens of times a day. Sometime later, I tracked him down while I was out in Vegas for a tournament. I learned he was at the tables and found out where he was staying. He opened the door having been on a bender, and on seeing me, the colour drained from his face. I said to him, 'I'm not leaving until you pay up'. Sure enough, he paid up and even though it wasn't much in the big scheme of things, it was a point of principle for me.

I needed to do it for my dad as well. The number of times he's told me to be careful, and I've replied, 'Yeah, yeah, yeah.' Then this one thing happened, and I couldn't face him until I'd got that money. If I'd failed, Dad would have never let it go.

While making sure the stakes were paid before each game began was a constant battle, it was also exciting, because we were seeing a return. Gradually, Matchroom Poker crept up on snooker and darts in terms of revenue, before finally overtaking them. We'd hit the game at a perfect time, but it was an immensely proud moment for us all. Eventually, poker was by far the most profitable department in the company's stable. We didn't simply luck out, however. We poured huge amounts of creativity into the formats we produced.

Perhaps my favourite was the 48-hour televised cash game. Inevitably, people were getting hammered and falling asleep at the table. It was brilliant to watch, and so popular because these games had stories unfolding through them. From the price of the buy-in to the size of the prize money pot or the duration of the games, we pushed the boundaries as far as we could. It was about ramping up the excitement and engagement, and providing nothing but value on every level for the customers.

Dad would always be questioning my plans to go bigger. He was naturally more cautious than me after decades in the business, but that was a good thing. Whenever he said, 'Steady now,' I heard out his reasons. It served to stress test every decision I made, and that would be rewarded when the outcome lived up to expectation.

Sometimes I'd have to take cash from the end of a tournament to bank the next day, which isn't something Dad encouraged, but there was no way round it. We'd finish filming late, and so I'd have no choice but to set off in the car with a hundred grand plus, which I then stashed under the bed before visiting the bank as they opened. That was almost part of the job, really. But that's what was driving my ambition, and it worked. However, there were times when I knew I had pushed things as far as they could go.

Around this time, the big online gaming companies began setting up accounts to aid the transfer of money. It was a last resort for me, because although it was legitimate, it could get messy. Before anyone sat down at the table, I wanted to see the money in the Matchroom bank account. Ultimately, that belonged to us and not the gaming company, which usually came under American jurisdiction.

As the game became more lucrative, players were transferring millions of dollars to each other via their online poker accounts. Every now and then, a player would request that he transfer their buy-in to my online account. This was rejected but as the buy-ins got bigger, it became a tempting solution to ensure we didn't get knocked. Before the start of one tournament two players requested they send the quarter of a million dollar buy-in to my poker account and we simply pay out the prize money via the same method. It sounded simple and I was pressed for time but I'd been reading that across the Atlantic the authorities were looking into tightening up legislation around such transactions between gaming accounts. With half a million quid at stake, I had to go with my instincts.

'I'm sorry,' I told them both. 'I can't do it.'

The two players weren't best pleased, and I felt bad for them.

Four hours later, as the game played out for the cameras, news broke that the American authorities had launched a formal investigation into the practice. This included the immediate freezing of all online gaming accounts. Had I taken the half a million in that way, I wouldn't have been able to cover the prize money. That was as close to a scare as I ever got in that game, but it proved to me that judgement is everything.

I took poker from a hunch that it could work for Matchroom, to turning over a million pounds a year. I spent most of the time in a darkened television studio as we filmed game after game, and I kept a close eye on every aspect. It was always fascinating to watch, because I'd become passionate about the game. Sometimes, I'd even travel to a tournament as a player in my own right.

It was at a World Poker Series in Las Vegas where I met the boxer Audley Harrison, and this changed everything. He was an Olympic gold medallist and a heavyweight contender with an impressive record, but by then his golden days were behind him. Unusually for a professional boxer, he'd taken control of his own career and effectively managed himself. He was a smart guy, but in my view fighters fight and promoters promote. Over the years, his prospects had dwindled until games such as poker provided more of a draw to him than a punchbag.

Audley's enthusiasm, personality and drive were still there, however, and that was evident to me when we were drawn at the same table in Vegas. I knew who he was, of course. Given my dad's business interest in the sport, although Matchroom weren't doing so much of it any more, I introduced myself as his son.

'So, do you look after the boxing?' Audley asked me, as we shook hands.

This was in 2007. Back then, Sky Sports was almost the only channel to cover fights, and it had lost a great deal of glamour and shine. It had also contracted to being a kind of cosy club, in which the broadcaster had a certain number of events that they divided between four promoters: Matchroom, Frank Warren, Kelly Maloney and Ricky Hatton. Nobody ever talked to each other – it was an unwritten arrangement, like slicing up a cake – and Matchroom would get a couple of fights in the same way as the others. As a result, there was no real competition or edge. On television, boxing had seen better days.

In a bid to liven things up a little, and appeal to the casual fan, Matchroom had put together a TV series called *Prizefighter*. Somehow, Dad had persuaded the British Boxing Board of Control to allow eight fighters to take part in four quarter-finals that were each judged on the best of three rounds of three minutes each. The winners would go onto the semis, and then the final, where the Prizefighter was crowned on the night. The hardcore fans thought it was a bit of a joke, but it had the same kind of appeal as Twenty20 cricket and ran for quite a few years.

As a show, *Prizefighter* was hungry for boxers and especially household names. So, when Audley Harrison asked me if I had any involvement with the sport at Matchroom, I did think I might be able to point him in the right direction. I couldn't blag an opportunity, like I had when I first started working. I was older, a little wiser, and frankly my experience at Matchroom was in one thing only.

'I do the poker,' I told him in all honesty.

'Yeah, but do you think you can get me a fight?'

Audley is a big, intense kind of guy. All of a sudden, I felt his hopes settle on my shoulder.

'I don't know, Audley. I don't really do the boxing.'

'Just give me the opportunity,' he said, as we talked. 'I still have so much to give.'

As a sales pitch, it was impressive. I'll give him that. He believed in himself and was absolutely convinced he still had a future in the ring. At the same time, as we talked, people were coming up to the table for selfies and autographs. It was the last thing I expected as we sat down at the poker table, but the only thing on my mind as we played. This guy had a profile.

'So, there's *Prizefighter*,' I told him. 'Why don't you go in for that?'

Audley made a face like the cards he'd been dealt weren't up to much.

'Nah,' he said. 'That's three rounds, right? It's a bit risky.'

'It's a great way back for you,' I said, coming right back at him as if he was a customer on a call in two minds about new windows. 'You also won Olympic gold with the same knockout round format. And if you won *Prizefighter*, I could probably get you a shot at the European championship, and after that, well, you know the big one from there.'

At that time, David Haye was the heavyweight world champion. I watched Audley Harrison's eyes light up as he said the name on my lips and considered what that would mean. At the same time, I quietly asked myself why the fuck I'd gone there again.

'You really think you could deliver on this for me?' he asked.

Honestly? I had no clue. Boxing was in my blood in so many ways. I'd been attending fights with my dad since I was eight years old. I knew every fighter, every record but when it came to guiding a fighter to the ultimate glory, I knew next to nothing. All I was really thinking was that bagging a boxer like Audley Harrison for *Prizefighter* would be a result for Matchroom. Anything beyond that was pie in the sky. If he won, I guessed we'd deal with the next problem then.

'Audley,' I said, as we exchanged contact details. 'I have a good feeling about this.'

After the game ended, I went back to my hotel feeling pumped. I called my dad to tell him about whom I'd met and our conversation.

'Audley Harrison?' he said dismissively, and I knew why. Dad was a promoter. He could never understand why a boxer would want to manage their own career, and become a self-promoter. The two roles didn't work together, and when Audley had made that move, my dad marked his card. 'What does he want?'

'He wants to fight, Dad. Everyone knows who he is, and he's asked me to represent him.'

I told him my plan to put him into *Prizefighter*, and the possibilities that could follow with the European championship and a shot at the World Title.

My dad said nothing for a moment after I'd finished. Finally he drew breath.

'Are you mad?' he asked. 'If you want to take on Audley, then be my guest. But you're on your own.'

While I always call Dad to share my news, I also value his

advice. I don't take it every time, but I register any note of caution he sounds. In this case, I thought perhaps I should simply drop the whole Harrison thing. It wasn't part of some grand plan of mine – I'd bumped into the geezer at a poker table. I'd gone and promised him something massively ambitious, at a time when I was riding an amazing wave with the poker. Why would I want to throw that away, I asked myself, standing at my hotel window overlooking the Vegas skyline at night.

Later that evening, the phone rang. It was Audley.

'Eddie, I've been thinking about everything you said,' he told me. 'I'm in!'

'Mate, you won't regret it,' I replied, while a small voice in my head said *fuck*!

Prizefighter was filmed in York Hall, an iconic venue for boxing in East London's Bethnal Green. It has a capacity of just over one thousand people. It's rich in atmosphere, a little rough around the edges, but a great site for a fight night. I love the place to bits, but when I flew home from Las Vegas, I had a bigger plan in mind.

I'd had time to think on the flight. I admit that when I saw Audley at the table, I thought of him as a boxer who had seen better days. But as the fans flocked around him, I realised he certainly wasn't forgotten. Then there was his passion. He wanted this return more than anything, and had entrusted that to me. I didn't want to let him down – nor did I want to disappoint myself or Matchroom, even if I did feel out of my depth. It meant that if I was going to get behind the guy, I'd have to do whatever it took to make it a success.

As a first step, there was no doubt in my mind that Audley was a big catch for *Prizefighter*. It would be the first heavyweight event with a major name, and I wanted to reflect that in the venue. As much as I liked York Hall, I needed a bigger stage. I also knew it would take some selling to bring my dad on board.

'You've booked what?' he said, when I told him about the ExCel Centre.

'It holds six thousand,' I told him. 'It's going to look epic.'

'It's going to be expensive,' he said, as if to focus my priorities. 'How much did you pay for that?'

'Twenty grand,' I replied, mindful that it was ten times what we paid for York Hall.

'Eddie, I've done a lot of boxing shows. It's easy to put on a fight that doesn't sell. *Prizefighter* is on live television. Think how it'll look if there's empty seats.'

'You just have to trust me, Dad, it'll be a sell-out. I know it.'

First and foremost, when it comes to boxing, I've always been a fan. I knew every stage in Audley's career before he introduced himself to me. Even though I thought his better days were behind him at the time, I could see he still had star value. Put that together with a popular show like *Prizefighter* and I was convinced we had a winner.

And we did it.

Shortly after the announcement, when the tickets went on sale at the ExCel Arena, we sold out every seat. We had Audley and seven other heavyweights on the bill for one night, and the buzz was incredible. When Dad sees that something's gone well, especially if it's against his better judgement, he recognises it. I love him for that. He's not too precious, and his enthusiasm for the fight matched mine.

It was one thing putting on the tournament in a bigger arena. I also wanted to make it feel like a special occasion. So, I made a couple of changes to the way things ran, which raised a few eyebrows. Firstly, in order to get everyone hyped, I hired a street dance act from *Britain's Got Talent* to perform in the ring at the top of the show. It looked amazing in rehearsal, but the director was having none of it.

'What the fuck is this?' he asked. 'I thought this was a fight.'

'It's Eddie's idea,' said my dad, who had also been shaking his head, but had my back on this. 'Let him do it.'

With the arena packed to the rafters, and the place buzzing. It was an unbelievable atmosphere. Having invested so much planning and *faith* into the night, I watched with a grin on my face. Then came the ring walk, which was where I had made another change.

Normally, the fighters walked on to some random background music. This time, I wanted them to choose their own track, and make it something that summed up their personality and ambition. I wanted it pumped around the arena so that everyone paid attention. This time, as I discovered when the music failed to play, the director was having none of it. The two boxers, whom I'd briefed to take their music as a cue, stood there in the wings looking confused. With six thousand people waiting for the show to begin, I ran out to the production trailer.

'Unless you play that music,' I told the director, 'then the fighters aren't walking.'

I wasn't bluffing. This was a *Prizefighter* show that had to stand head and shoulders over every other show that had gone before. For that to happen, I could not afford to compromise on the vision I had set out. The director found himself looking into my eyes, which had narrowed, and probably registered the fact that I had yet to blink.

Twenty seconds later, the first fighter came on to his ring walk music.

Hand on heart, it was a memorable show for me for all

the right reasons. Every hope I had for that night came true. Not only that, Audley Harrison fought his way through every round to win the tournament. The place went absolutely nuts and I jumped into the ring to congratulate Audley. For the *Prizefighter* champion, I was reminded there and then, this was only the beginning.

'We did it, Eddie! Phase one!' Audley was dripping in sweat but elated, and I could see he was already thinking several steps ahead of me. 'Now we fight for the European, right?'

Frankly, I had surprised myself by making *Prizefighter* such a success. I knew I had the passion and the commitment to give it my best shot, but this went beyond all expectation. I should've gone home and celebrated hard. Instead, I went back and had to give myself a proper talking to. There was no way I could throw in the towel now – I had to deliver on a promise. The EBU had approved the European title fight between Audley and Michael Sprott, who had defeated Harrison in 2007. It proved to be expensive to secure the fight, but we set it up.

The fight took place in 2010 at Alexandra Palace in North London. It was a chance for me to build on the *Prizefighter* experience, where I had learned not to compromise. We sold about five thousand tickets, which was reasonable. My dad felt we'd spent too much when he looked at the books, but by then I'd begun thinking ahead. If Audley defied expectation and won, he would have a shot at the World Heavyweight Title. With Matchroom on a percentage, potentially we were looking at serious money but more importantly we were back in the bigtime.

'As long as you know what you're doing,' my dad smirked. It was as much of a warning, as it was encouragement.

But by then we were on a roll.

Come fight night, watching from the front row, I wished I could've been anywhere else but there. After suffering a pectoral injury early in the fight, Audley lost nearly every round. In the build-up, I'd found my voice with the media. I'd been drumming up belief that this was only a stepping stone for my guy, and once he beat Sprott, we could be looking at an all-British World Heavyweight dust-up; one of the greatest fights in history. I knew full well that Audley had his critics, but I hadn't paid them any attention.

My dad was sitting next to me. With two minutes to go before the final bell, and Audley reeling with every punch and jab, he gave me a nudge in the arm.

'You alright, son?'

'I can't believe it,' I said, trying to keep up a brave face in front of all these people. 'All he had to do was beat this geezer and we'd be in for the Heavyweight World Title.'

My dad glanced at me side on.

'Son, when the bell goes, we're both going to get in the ring. I'll congratulate Sprott and you commiserate with Audley. It's the right thing to do. You do it like a man and then you move on.'

'Fuck that,' I said, as Sprott continued to smash him. 'I ain't getting in the ring.'

'You gotta do it.'

'No way, Dad.'

Seconds later, when nobody expected it, Audley landed a massive left hand on Sprott's chin and sparked him clean out. It took a moment for me to register before I was up on my feet and scrambling between the ropes.

'Audley! You did it!' I cried, as he stood there in absolute astonishment. 'I'd always knew it would come! I never lost faith!' Underneath it all I was thinking that we got a gift from the gods.

The guy had lost nearly every single round. But that didn't

matter. When the referee finally held Audley Harrison's arm aloft, we raised the roof in celebration.

At the post-fight press conference that evening, Audley faced the crowd of journalists and claimed that God had told him he would win this fight.

'But Audley,' one said, 'before that knockout, you lost every round.'

'What matters is the result,' I intervened, and then found a camera lens. 'David Haye, this is a message for you,' I went on, because I figured as Audley's promoter I needed at least to make all the right noises. 'The public wants to see you in the ring together. This day will come . . .'

I didn't think Haye would bite. Audley had picked up the European strap, but everyone could see that it was down to a hail-mary punch. That didn't stop Audley from pressing me to sort it out. He really believed that this was his moment, and I had that responsibility on my shoulders to end this job. I couldn't go to my old man and ask him to fix this – it was all on me.

Then one day my phone rang, and a representative for David Haye asked if Audley and I would fly out to Vegas that weekend for a meeting. Haye and his people would be there, and hoped to hammer out the terms for what promised to be the fight of a lifetime.

I'll always be very fond of Audley, and that whole episode in our lives. One thing I'll always say about him is that he understood the dynamics of the business. At a time when I was setting up fights by the seat of my pants, I learned a lot from him. It gave me the confidence to jump on a plane with him for that meeting. I knew how to hold my own in a negotiation, but the finer points of a boxing contract were still new to me. I couldn't let that show.

'So, we want the blue corner,' Haye's representative said, 'and obviously second ring walk.'

'Yeah, yeah. That's understandable,' I said, thinking, *what the fuck are they talking about*, and looking to Audley to back me up.

After the meeting, Audley and I went through every clause in that contract. It was a steep learning curve for me, but I wanted to make the right call for him. In the end, we signed it in Las Vegas

'I've done it, Dad!' I told him. 'I've got the Haye fight! It's on!'

My dad wanted to know how much we stood to make, and whistled when I told him.

'I can't believe it!' he said. 'Audley's going to get battered, but you done well.'

'He's going to win!' I insisted, and I really believed it. Despite the chance victory in his last fight, Audley was so endearing that I had to get behind him. He's a mountain of a man, who is brimming with positivity, and I really admired that in him. I was convinced he'd be victorious, and it was my responsibility to exceed all expectation as the fight's promoter.

'People told him he would never get an education, and he went and got a degree. People told him he was too old to start amateur boxing, but he went and won Olympic gold.'

I was addressing a cluster of press microphones, which was becoming an increasingly regular occurrence ahead of the fight, and talking up Audley Harrison as if he was the saviour of British boxing.

'People told him that he'd never be a world champion, but on the thirteenth of November 2010, his destiny will come true.'

I thought I sounded great. Behind the scenes, people were

coming up to me and saying, 'Are you being serious? Haye will savage him!'

'I'm telling you,' I'd say, and I meant it, because I believed it myself, and that meant every word came from the heart. 'Audley's going to win.'

Audley himself was singing from the same hymn sheet. He was absolutely convinced that he could take down David Haye. There wasn't a single moment in the run-up to that fight where he thought he would be anything other than victorious. The conviction was incredible, and I fed off it.

When we announced the fight, it was greeted widely as a joke. Like my dad, everyone thought Haye would completely outclass Harrison. But as the date drew closer, and Audley and I continued to share our belief in the press, the odds began to represent a close fight. *Boxing News* put out an edition with Audley's face on the front and the headline: *He can't . . . can he?*

Even my dad bought into it in the end. One day I overheard him in his office. He was on the phone, talking to a journalist, and said outright that he believed Audley Harrison was going to be world champion. That's when I figured that I had done my job.

The fight between Haye and Harrison was set to take place at Manchester Arena. It was massive, with over 20,000 tickets sold and half a a million pay-per-view (PPV) sales on Sky. I was physically shaking at the pre-fight press conference. I kept my hands out of view and started talking. I don't remember much about what I said, apart from turning to the reigning world champ and telling him he had no chin. Like David Haye himself, who took it with good grace, I imagine the seasoned journalists were thinking what a twat I was, but to be fair I was delivering what they needed to keep us in the headlines all the way to fight night.

'This is it, Audley,' I told him in his dressing room. We could hear music pulsing through the walls from the main arena, and the chatter and hum of expectation from a legion of fans that had packed out the place. 'It's time to achieve the dream,' I urged him. 'Go out there and become world champion!'

Audley's quite a religious guy. With his gloves on, he went into a little huddle with his team and they prayed. 'This is my night of destiny,' I heard him growl as they broke apart, sounding totally focused and massively pumped. As his people assembled to set out for the ring walk, all I could think was, *Jesus, he's going to smash Haye!*

When Audley's ring walk music filled the arena – 'In the Air Tonight' by Phil Collins – I couldn't help but look around as we walked out with him. As a kid, I'd stood in the ring to hold belts for fighters, but this was different. Even before we reached the centre of the arena, I could sense people looking at me, and I even heard some saying, 'That's the guy. That's the promoter, Eddie Hearn.' Nobody went, 'That's Barry's son,' which was a first.

With Audley in the ring first, as per the terms of the contract, it was the turn of the self-proclaimed 'Hayemaker' to make his entrance. To the sound of 'Ain't No Stopping Us Now', the spotlights swept across the arena to shine on David Haye. Maybe it was the dramatic lighting or the way he faced the crowd, but somehow he looked completely different than at the press conference. He stood there imperiously, ripped to shreds like a Greek god, and I thought *fuck*.

With all eyes on his opponent, Audley Harrison stood alone in the ring and quite possibly thought the same thing.

Looking down at him from the ring, I watched Haye prowl past me and climb up onto the apron. He saluted the crowd, who went wild. Then he glared at Audley, who seemed to shrink away. From where I was sitting, it looked as if he completely froze.

'So, what do you reckon?' my dad asked from the seat beside me.

'I don't know,' I said, aware that all the confidence I'd brought with me had just disappeared.

From the bell for the first round to the end of the second, neither fighter threw a proper punch. Haye was clearly up for it, but Harrison literally kept him at arm's length with no willingness to engage. It looked to me as if Haye couldn't work out what was going on with this guy who had come for his crown. Whether he expected a few initial jabs from range or a gamble on the inside, it didn't materialise. Even the referee reminded the pair that some boxing would be good. When the crowd started booing, I felt sick to my stomach.

In the third round, Haye's patience seemed to run out. Suddenly he launched in and started teeing off at will. Audley looked more like a human punchbag. The sheer power and ferocity of those shots sent Audley crashing to the canvas. I looked at my man, flat out on his back, and then wondered if he made the wisest move by struggling back onto his feet. Naturally Haye came straight back in with his big lead right and finished it, just as the first missiles from the rowdy crowd sailed over the ropes.

'Go on, son,' my dad said, as the arena echoed to the sound of booing. 'Get in the ring!'

I just froze – I really didn't want to get in there.

This time my dad demanded my full attention.

'Get in that ring and do the right thing. You were quick enough to do so last time!'

I climbed through the ropes, hoping I could hide in the throng of people now filling the canvas. Slumped in his corner,

Audley looked completely defeated. His team were consoling him, saying he'd been unlucky. As the jeers and booing continued to build, all I knew was that I had to get him out of the arena before things turned ugly.

Together with his security team, we made our way to the tunnel at the back. On the way, people were yelling abuse. All we could do was stay close to each other and keep our heads down. With the tunnel a matter of feet away, I caught the eye of a pissed off fan, who was staring at me from the stands.

'Hearn!' he yelled at me, and the buzz I'd felt earlier at being recognised in my own right, and not as my dad's son, was gone. 'You are a *shit* promoter!'

'What happened?' I asked Audley, as we prepared to make our way back to his dressing room, but he had little to say. Without a doubt, it was one of the worst nights of my life. I had to deal with Audley in the dressing room, who insisted he didn't have a chance to get going, and encourage him to face the post-fight press conference. Frankly, it was humiliating. It felt as if even the media thought I was a joke. Having pumped them for so long about Audley's potential, I wanted to head home and hide away.

Towards two o'clock in the morning, having finished my interviews, packed off Audley, thanked my team, and dealt with the post-fight duties, my chance came to leave. By then, Manchester Arena was pretty much deserted. With my head down, I made my way around a service corridor, heading for the exit. I felt so low in that moment and wanted nothing more to do with boxing. Having carved a name for myself in poker, and made a success of it, this had been nothing but a rollercoaster of ups and downs before the whole thing came off the rails.

I was so lost in thought, feeling sorry for myself, that I

looked up with a start on seeing someone else in the corridor. The figure was heading towards me, striding with a purpose. Then I recognised the man, and responded probably as Audley Harrison had when the spotlights fell upon his opponent.

It was David Haye.

In that moment of recognition, all the taunting and grief I had conjured up for the benefit of the media went through my mind. *You've got no chin. You're overrated.* I had really given it to him.

I braced myself for some kind of comeback. David is an imposing figure, and I felt like some try-hard who had done nothing but wind him up for weeks. For a second I thought about keeping my gaze to the floor and hoping I could walk on by. Instead, perhaps thinking what my dad would do, I looked up as he came close.

In response, Haye grinned at me and winked.

'Well done,' he said, as we passed. 'That was brilliant!'

'Yeah,' I said, and covered for my shock by sounding like this was the outcome I had always expected.

It was a moment of sheer relief, and I dwelled on it during my drive home. All I could think was that the defending world champion had sealed his reputation in front of a record crowd and pay-per-view numbers. Yes, he'd had to put up with me trash-talking him, but it was all part of a deal that had paid out millions for him. That night I went to bed a troubled man and clung to this one consoling thought.

The next day, I went into the Matchroom offices. There, I prepared to face my dad and the rest of the team.

'Ed, that was the worst fight ever. He didn't throw a punch. What happened?'

Like Audley, I had no comeback. All I could do was take the punches. Having drummed up so much enthusiasm and high hopes, and sold the event to the best of my abilities, I felt like a con artist.

At lunch, I headed out to the local café. I went there all the time and, of course, I'd been talking up the fight for ages. I arrived at peak time and the place was packed. As soon as I opened the door, everyone turned around and the noise inside died.

In silence, I made my way to the counter and asked for a chicken salad sandwich. The guy serving noted my order, but stared at me.

'Eddie, I paid fifteen quid to watch that fight. We all did!' he added, gesturing around the café. 'And we're never going to get that money back.'

I'd spent a lot of time apologising that day, and this was no exception. With my sandwich in a bag, and no appetite to eat it, I turned and hurried out with everyone glaring at me. As I told my dad that afternoon, I was finished with boxing. The poker was lower profile and easier in every way.

That week, whenever the phone rang, I didn't exactly jump to take the call. I'd had enough of defending my fighter to the press. There wasn't much that I could say, anyway. So, when the boxing trainer Tony Sims rang me – I knew him through my dad – I was surprised by the question he put to me.

'Are Matchroom making a move back into boxing?' he asked.

'Mate, did you see the fight?'

'I did,' he confirmed. 'And I was wondering whether you'd be interested in representing one of my guys?'

'What?' My first thought was this had to be a wind-up.

'Darren Barker. You know?'

'The European middleweight champion,' I said, still stunned at the course of this conversation. Despite my experience as a promoter, I knew my boxing. 'Are you serious?'

'Eddie, you just took Audley Harrison to a World Title shot. If you can promote him, you can promote *anyone*!'

One week later, having signed Darren because I couldn't resist it, I took another call from the father of Kell Brook, a quality fighter and future welterweight champion. He took the same view as Darren, and in due course his son also joined the Matchroom stable. When the call came from Carl Froch, a top-level fighter and the WBC super-middleweight champ, I realised that perhaps this wasn't the end of my time as a boxing promoter after all.

Yes, I had been through a trial by fire, but with that experience under my belt and belief in me from some of the best British fighters, I was all in now. With the drive, passion and ambition to succeed that had been instilled in me at such an early age, and sheer relentless energy, I recognised that I had taken a vital first step into a career that would enable me to create a legacy.

ROUND 3 – KEY TAKEAWAYS

- Always stay ambitious and think big. If you're going to be thinking anything, why not think big? If people aren't calling your ideas crazy, then maybe you aren't thinking big enough.

- Pay attention to details and never make the same mistake twice. It's the little details that can make big things happen.

- You can never ever stop learning because life never stops teaching; it's the one thing we all have in common. You'll never know at what point the skills you have acquired will be called upon to succeed. The more skills, the more knowledge, the more chance to overcome a problem.

- Judgement is everything. Make sure you stand by your gut feeling. I've lost count of the number of times I've analysed a decision and reverted to my gut feeling, but never without analysis.

Part Two

HOW TO SUCCEED

Round 4

PLAY THE HAND YOU'RE
DEALT

Before we get into the nitty gritty, we've got to wipe the slate clean. I'm sure there will be many people in different positions reading this book. Some may be happy, some unfulfilled and others trying to find their way in life. One thing we all have in common, however, is the search for happiness. Ultimately, all that really matters is where we finish the journey and how content we are in getting there.

But whatever our destination, every single one of us has to begin somewhere – and our starting point will always be unique.

Seize the Opportunity

As I've already said, my dad grew up on a council estate in Dagenham. His dad was a bus driver. He carved out an empire for himself with a sharp brain, big balls and a lot of luck. I was born into money. I share my parents' working-class values, but there's no doubt I've had a leg-up. I'll be up front here and say I'm jealous of my dad's start in life. Sometimes we go for a walk around the grounds of the house where my parents now live. It's truly incredible. He's got four hundred acres of field, woodland and lakes. We'll be talking business, when suddenly he will break off and look around.

'I can't believe this,' he'll say, and his astonishment at what he's achieved is compelling. I can't get my head around how that must feel, because I didn't start with nothing. I never experienced the struggle he went through in the beginning. Instead, my challenge has been about making my own name for myself and turning 'Barry Hearn's son' into 'Eddie Hearn's dad'. In my situation, based on where I began, the only way I can be judged is by the level to which I take the family business.

To this aim, I've been viciously driven to outperform my old man and continue the legacy he's built. I couldn't simply take over because I was his boy and hope for the best. I needed to know what I was doing to get to the top of that game without rest. Today, I constantly set myself bigger goals and I fight tooth and nail to achieve them.

In sharing the story of how I became a boxing promoter, and shook up the sport in the process, I wanted to be brutally honest. It's an essential quality when it comes to pursuing success. It creates clarity of mind and invites respect. You have to be up front with people if you expect them to be the same with you, and my dad has shown me that is the most effective way to get business done. So, I set out to account for the years that shaped my values, attitude and outlook on life as transparently as I could. I experienced success but also crushing humiliation, and learned a great deal from it all.

I also wanted to be completely up front about the fact that I was born into wealth. People give me stick for it all the time, but it's the hand that I was dealt. It shaped me, of course, but not as you might imagine. The fact is I do not take money for granted, or assume that privilege sets me apart in any way, and I have my dad to thank for that.

As a five-year-old facing my old man as he prepared to unleash a cricket ball with his full force, it didn't matter what kind of background I came from. Unless I summoned the right qualities and faced it head on, I was going to get out. That was my starting point in life, and my dad gave me no other choice for good reason. I never got a soft ball from him, and I'm grateful, because those are the ones that lead to complacency. This has stayed with me, even now. You have to work hard.

Even now, a generation later, my dad still plays the same game. I'm happily married to my wife, Chloe, and we have two lovely daughters. When my eldest picked up a table tennis bat recently, her grandfather was delighted.

'Before we start,' he said to her, 'you need to know that I will not let you win.'

Dad's in his seventies now, but he hasn't lost any of his competitive edge.

'Alright, whatever,' my daughter said, which kind of delighted me.

'If you win,' her grandad said, 'it's because you deserve it.'

So, they play every week. She's probably faced him across the net about forty times now, and never claimed a single game. Even so, she's rising to the challenge. I appreciate that many people will think this is such a strange mentality. *Just let her win*, someone will say to him, but he outright refuses.

'She will beat me when she's ready,' he insists, and at the time of writing that moment is not too far away.

When it comes to seizing opportunity, our qualities as individuals will determine what we do with it. From tidying up the office stationery cupboard in your first job to running a boxing division at Matchroom and turning it into a success, opportunities present themselves throughout our lives and careers. What matters is how you execute them, and the amount of passion you put in, because that doesn't go unnoticed. Achieving greatness might require many other things, and time is often a factor, but grasping that chance in the first place demands fundamentals that will always remain the same. In making the most of an opportunity, there's no place for bitterness or complacency, laziness or arrogance.

We've all got our problems, but we still have to be the best we can be. I wasn't born to take our business to another level. Fortunately, Dad made it his mission in life to raise a son who recognised the value of hard work, sweat and tears. He wanted me to be dangerous. When I finally joined the family firm, I did so at a time when I felt my resumé and experience would have earned me the place on their own – I knew I was ready, as did my dad. He had wanted me to come in only when the moment was right. I needed to earn my stripes in my own way.

Having squandered my early schooling a little, I set out into the workplace knowing I couldn't afford to miss any chances. My journey, as I hope I've set out, was about grabbing those openings when they came – even if they weren't meant for me – and then setting out to do my level best with them. Not everything resulted in triumph. I'll never forget that sending off I received when escorting Audley to the tunnel after he got spanked by Haye. As stinging as it might have been, it's moments like those that have defined who I am. They fuelled my commitment to strive constantly for success.

So, whatever your background, no matter where you've come from, let's set that aside and focus on the cards you've been dealt. Rich or poor, privileged or otherwise, how you play them depends on the values that shape you. That determines what you do with opportunity, whether it's in your gift, or you create it from absolutely nothing.

On Purpose and Passion

None of us are born to be successful. With the right qualities it's something we fight to achieve, but it's never going to be an easy journey. It demands that we align every aspect of our lives to pursuing that ultimate goal. From a personal ambition to realising a professional dream, you've got to want it like nothing else, and be prepared to make sacrifices along the way. It might be a destination, or simply a direction of travel. In my mind, there is no point in my future where I plan to sit back and say I have arrived.

For me, the journey never ends. Once I hit a target, I'm onto the next, and that has to be bigger and bolder than the last. My concept of success is to keep building on it, but that still requires a motivating force. So, whatever you set your sights upon, it's vital that you understand what's driving you.

It's no secret that I have a chip on my shoulder. I get enough grief, on social media and in the real world, about the fact that I come from money. Even my dad calls me Silver Spoon! When I formed Matchroom Golf, people immediately assumed my dad had handed it to me like a brand new car. The truth was I'd had to bust my nuts to create that opportunity. It was a Matchroom venture in name only. Everything else was down to me.

Naturally, it didn't stop the critics, but I no longer view

that kind of thing as a negative. If anything, when people make assumptions about me based on my background, I'm driven to prove them wrong. In the same way, I'm determined to build on my dad's successes and take things even further. That's what gets me out of bed in the morning. It's the hunger that enables me to stay sharp, focused and positive about the future ahead.

When I joined Matchroom, my ambitions were on the rise. I had poker in mind and an absolute commitment to making it the biggest earner for the company. At the same time, having achieved so much and with three decades on me, my dad's ambitions were coming down. This was no measure of his drive – it's a fact of life. But it meant he would sometimes hear out my plans and strike a note of caution. I'd hate to be proven wrong by him, and so I'd set about pursuing a goal with everything in my power to make it work.

With poker, I proposed televised matches with a level of prize money that made his eyes water. I believed we needed to offer a dramatic amount to bring in both players and viewers. I always heard out the reasons behind his caution, of course, and took it on board, and in a way that made extra sure I didn't regret it.

Audley's appearance on *Prizefighter* was perhaps the first time I took my dad seriously out of his comfort zone. Dad would have settled with staging the fight at Bethnal Green's York Hall. I knew it could be much bigger than that and pushed for the ExCel Centre. Can you imagine the humiliation if I'd messed that up? My dad would never have let me forget it! Failure was not an option. I was *driven* to make it a success.

What's great is that Dad also recognises when I've made the

right call. It's been a question of building trust, I suppose, and I've worked hard to earn it. Where once he'd warn, 'I don't think you should do that,' now he's more likely to hear out my proposal for a show and say, 'Fuck me, you're mad, but you're the master.' It's good to hear. Subconsciously, I know I'm always trying to prove myself to my dad and that cuts to the heart of what drives me. I have to be successful on my own terms, and take things to a level above and beyond his own achievements.

Asking yourself what keeps you motivated might well involve some soul-searching. It isn't necessarily about striking it rich. People do incredible things for all kinds of reasons, but I can only tell you what keeps me driven. Thanks to my dad, my motivation has been in development since I was a kid.

With a bunch of boxing programmes under my arm, I couldn't just stand there and hope to sell a copy – I needed to work hard at persuading fans to part with their cash. From the commission I could earn selling advertising space, to persuading people they wanted to buy double glazing, it demanded determination from me. I had to want to make a success of it.

The skills these things required took time for me to master, but the hunger had to be there from the start. Otherwise, I'd have packed it in after I found myself cut off on a call as soon as I said I wanted to talk about windows.

If purpose drives the pursuit of success, passion will ensure you put your heart and soul into it. Let's say you're selling vacuum cleaners. You know damn well the range doesn't pick up very well, or the dust bag splits when half full. It doesn't matter if you're the best salesperson in the world, if the product is crap and you're not that into it, then you're never going be truly successful. The passion you would need to persuade a customer this vacuum cleaner is the dog's bollocks? You'd have to put on an act.

You're not being honest with the person you're selling to, and chances are they'll see through you. Nor are you being honest to yourself. My dad has a saying that we often use at Matchroom. If there's no passion then there's no point, and I really believe in that. Everything I do has to come from the heart. It means I love what I do and the more energy I put into it, the better it gets.

It also makes selling so much easier.

The vacuum cleaner manufacturer you represent? They've redesigned their product line. Now you're selling kit that's better than anything out there. It purrs like a kitten, leaves your floors and carpets like new, and the dust bag is made from an indestructible material. All of a sudden you've got several kinds of talking points, and you mean every word you say. Your enthusiasm is infectious, and the sales will reflect that.

I don't sell vacuum cleaners. I put on boxing shows, but I live for the sport and love it. I've grown up around boxers, and misguidedly I even fancied my chances as a contender for one very brief period. I've built my career on being outside the ring, not in it. Even so, I share the same fire in my belly as the fighters who put their lives on the line when the first bell rings.

With purpose and passion, I am driven to stage the very best shows that I can. The fact is I'm a fan as much as a promoter. For me, the two are inseparable. I want people to experience something truly special at my fights, because that's what I would expect in their shoes. We're talking about a spectacle that's value for money, which they'll talk about for ages afterwards and will come back for more of. That's not something I could ever dial in.

We'll return to purpose and passion, because they are central to success. Before we go any further, however, it's vital that you pinpoint what these qualities mean to your life or business. We're not talking about two things you can simply switch on here. Both have to be completely authentic. So dig deep, because finding them is the surest way to maximise your potential.

Motivate, Don't Hate

I used to have a tendency to resent people for being successful. Sometimes at school I wanted others to fail. I'm embarrassed by it now, but at the time if the spotlight fell on some student for their achievements I would stew on it. Why? Firstly, because I badly wanted to be a winner myself. That had been drilled into me by my dad. It's just that when you want something that intensely, it can put you off trying in case you fall short.

Then there was my background, which was the last word in success, only I hadn't earned it.

As far as my mates were concerned, being the son of Barry Hearn meant I lived the dream. I didn't need to achieve because I was already there. I went home to a mansion and got driven around in a flash car. Success was all around me, but I was born into it – and that's hardly an achievement. If a classmate worked their nuts off and got top marks in the classroom, or was considered to be man of the match on the playing fields, they had rightfully earned praise for their success. It was the kind of praise I wanted for myself. The difference was that nobody ever clapped me on the back for a job well done in being a silver spoon kid.

I was young at the time, of course. I was learning about myself, my place in the world and what I wanted to do with my life. Even so, I let my resentment of success get out of hand at times. I could be on a school team for cricket or rugby, and actively will a teammate to screw up so he didn't get all the limelight. How crazy is that? Our best batsman could walk out to bat, and I'd hope that he wouldn't get as many runs as me. Even if that meant our team lost the game, I struggled watching others shine.

It could be said that I was massively competitive from an early age, and there is some truth in that, but my background weighed heavily on my shoulders back then. I hadn't come to realise that we all start from different places, and that life is about levels. Fate does not determine what level you end up. How far you take things depends on your motivation, goals, commitment and drive. I was too young to recognise that at the time.

As a result, I developed a negative mentality. When someone did well, I couldn't find it in myself to share their joy. While others might get involved, exchanging high fives or slapping them on the back for a goal or a try, my congratulations would be hollow. But if that same player smashed a ball over the crossbar, or lost possession of the rugby ball, it would mean I may get the chance at individual glory.

Frank Lampard went to my school. He was in the year above me. He also had a famous dad; the footballer of the same name. So I was gutted when Frank Jr got picked to join the youth team at West Ham. How come he was allowed a break? Some bitter kids said it must've been down to his old man, and even I chimed in. That was how I saw life at school. Today, I look back and barely recognise myself. I'm in admiration at Frank's achievements. He made all the sacrifices to get there and I'm genuinely thrilled for him.

There's no place for negativity in life. It's a waste of time. It fuels insecurity and brings further misery. It achieves *nothing*. Now, I wish my competitors every success and happiness, and I mean it. There's a lot to be said for sharing positive energy, especially when people least expect it. Just don't confuse positivity with happiness. Ant Middleton once told me this, and he's right. They are two completely different things. It's also difficult to be positive all the time. I try, but I do have a tendency to be pessimistic sometimes, to avoid that crushing disappointment should things go wrong.

The fact is I'm rarely happy with my work, because I'm constantly pushing at those margins where I can improve. My positive thinking can also be tested if I'm in a bad situation, or things don't look good, and small mistakes in my work *consume* me. Even so, it can never be just a mantra to me, or something I can choose to adopt when it suits. Today, positivity has to be at the heart of my work ethic.

So, what turned me from someone who resented success in others to someone who celebrates it? I guess I grew into myself. If I wanted to achieve, then it was down to me to go out and earn it the same as anyone else. Calling name after name in the phone book as a double-glazing salesman taught me I could be resilient, and that was something I built on. Confidence soon followed as I talked to more customers, and with that came the buzz of securing a lead.

As I worked out what I was good at and how I could do better, I started going easier on the people around me. I became less jealous of success and learned to recognise that when someone has worked hard to achieve it, that deserves congratulations.

Today, I'm even happy for my business competitors when they do well. It doesn't make me bitter. What's the point? If anything, being aware of what their hard work has brought them might sharpen my focus to do better myself. It's a win all round.

Age doesn't guarantee you'll become a more positive person. What can change you for the better are the experiences you go through in life. They're what can make you understand that negativity is a disease. It's toxic! If you want to get on, and be your best, it's never going to happen if your priority lies in tearing other people down. I have only to look at social media to see that kind of attitude in action.

Let's say I post a link to a video of a recent chat I've had with a boxer. Fortunately, I'm mostly talking to fans. They'll be hyped, happy to see it, and it might even kick start a healthy, lively conversation about that fighter's form or future. Even so, I guarantee there'll be comments such as, 'It's alright for you, Eddie, in your expensive suit . . . sitting in your big house.'

Now, this kind of crap doesn't bother me. I've read it all before. Taking offence or worrying about it is a waste of my time and energy, but more importantly what is it doing for the person who posted it? They're *seething*; consumed by their own negative energy. They might say it's only a stupid comment that means nothing, but they took the time to think it up and write it down. And I'm sad to say that those are the people who will not get on in life. I look at those comments and feel pity. It's all noise, achieving nothing.

It's possible to change a negative outlook, of course, and I hope that maturity will make that happen for my online critics, but first they have to recognise the possibilities that open up when we look at the world through a positive lens. To those people, I'd say walk away from social media, go offline and enjoy the fresh air. Think about those dreams and ambitions you've been hiding from by throwing mud at those who strive. Figure out what's important to you – that thing you want to achieve – and when that spark comes, make it happen.

Positivity is a motivating force, not just for you on your path to success, but the people around you. Combined with purpose and passion, you'll never look back as positive energy goes where energy flows.

A Winning Mindset

My dad has a very simple outlook on life and business. It comes down to his concept of mindset, which is all about winning. You put 110 per cent into everything, and come out on top. That's it. End of story. No excuses. Simply taking part – that thing we're supposed to encourage in our children – it doesn't register for him.

It makes me laugh when I try to picture my dad being like that with me when I was a kid. 'Son, no matter how you get on today, I am proud of you . . .' That kind of thing. He never said it! There was no gentle, encouraging talk. Instead, he'd look me in the eye and bark, 'Get out there, Eddie, and nail those runs!' as if my life depended on it – and he could be brutal in his honesty.

Take football, which I enjoyed, but was no Frank Lampard. My dad would take me home after a match and he'd rubbish my performance on the pitch. 'You turn like an oil tanker . . . it takes you half an hour to get going!' and naturally that had a huge influence in shaping my mindset. I don't look back on those times and think he could've been a bit kinder. It didn't knock my confidence as you might expect, because he also had this way of focusing my attention on the rewards that were out there if I got better. We still laugh about those times to this day. It's how we were as father and son, but without a doubt I share his relentless dedication to the pursuit of winning.

As a father myself, I took my daughter to a school hockey match recently. Before the game started, I crouched down to be on her level and began my pep talk.

'Right. What you got to do is get the ball early and drive it home,' I urged her, 'because you're in a strong team and stand a good chance of coming out on top.'

That's when my wife intervened with a hand on my shoulder.

'What Dad means to say is that you've done really well to get in the team, and as long as you play your best, nothing else matters.'

'Yeah, that's right,' I mumbled after a moment, as if I'd been reminded of something important. 'Listen to your mother.'

To be successful, you have to know what makes you tick. You need to be aware of how you respond to a challenge, which defines your mindset. I used to give up at school if I didn't understand something straight away. Now, if I know that if I'm facing a massive undertaking to get a big show staged, I need to break it down into achievable goals and then work tirelessly at ticking my way through the list.

Consider the negative drivers as well. I'm fearful of failure, but that doesn't mean I avoid the challenge. Quite the opposite, in fact. I go the extra length to make a hundred per cent sure that I succeed. Through my eyes, failure has consequences. As a schoolkid, the prospect of failing used to stop me from trying and would leave me resentful of those who achieved. Now, with age and experience on my side, that fear motivates me to shift up a gear and get the job done. It's no longer a monster in my eyes. I've harnessed it as an energy.

As I see it, fear can be a positive force when it comes to shaping mindset. I didn't relish the prospect of my dad telling me where I went wrong on the pitch when I was younger. On the upside, it drove me to raise my game. In the same way, I often wish I could be as hardline with my own kids, to raise their awareness that for better or worse, actions have consequences.

'That's it!' I'll tell them, if they've been messing about. 'You've lost your phones until tomorrow!'

They'll hand them over, but there's no real remorse and that's down to me.

'I don't know why you bother,' my wife will say, as I stash the phones in a drawer. 'You'll hand them back in half an hour.'

We all try to do the right thing as parents. Sometimes, I wish I could be better. In business, however, I don't allow myself the space to be left thinking like that. I want to look back at a show and know that 110 per cent went into it. That winning mindset breeds all manner of values that are vital for success. I'm confident in what I do, go above and beyond to deliver, and surround myself with people who share the same work ethic. It's been with me since I was a kid, and means I don't flinch on stepping out of my comfort zone.

The same mentality saw me take Audley Harrison from a poker table to the fight with Haye. Yes, I was learning as I went along, but I seized that challenge and faced it head on. Even though the outcome of that fight made me feel briefly like a failure, when the phone started ringing I realised that I had earned success from it in other ways.

By 2011, it meant I had a growing stable of respected fighters and a mindset that would stop at nothing but the win. I also found myself in the role of promoter at a time when British boxing felt as if it had seen better days. Growing up, attending fights with my old man, the shows had some glamour and dazzle. They felt exciting. Dangerous. With the Haye/Harrison fight, I had demonstrated to my dad that the appetite for big boxing was still out there. It only needed someone to deliver it.

As I saw the situation, as a newcomer to boxing promotion I had the opportunity to shake things up. I looked at what the other promoters were doing, where the televised fights were carved up between them without anyone feeling they had to outshine everyone else, and I thought I could do better. Having made a success of poker, and with the strength and structure of the Matchroom business, I was absolutely convinced that I had what it takes to breathe new life into the sport.

Others in my situation might not have been so bold. They may well have kept their head down and aimed at jostling for position among the established promoters, or settled for pecking at their crumbs. Not me. I had a family business and a legacy to grow, as well as a reputation for taking things further than my dad had ever dreamed.

The opportunity was mine for the taking. I possessed the

purpose, the passion and the positivity, along with a mindset to get the job done. Now I had to prove to the powers that be who put boxing on our televisions that I could deliver on a vision.

ROUND 4 – KEY TAKEAWAYS

- Keep life simple – happiness is the ultimate goal, of course, but searching for it can also be one of the biggest causes of unhappiness! The best way to find it is not to search for it, but to create it.

- When it comes to seizing opportunities, our qualities as individuals will determine what we do with it. The doors of opportunity are always locked, but you will never know until you try to open them. One day they will open, and you have to be ready to walk through them and take your chance. Nothing is more expensive than a missed opportunity.

- None of us are born to be successful. It's never going to be an easy journey regardless of where you start. You can't inherit passion, drive and a relentless work ethic.

- To be successful, you have to understand what your definition of success is and you should define it on your own terms. It's not universal and only you can set the bar.

Round 5

THE WILL TO WIN

Unless you're driven to win, I'm really not sure how successful you can be. That's the bottom line. One thing I would say is that I've met some hungry fuckers who are desperate to win and it can lead to a lonely life. To be truly great you have to be selfish, almost horrible at times. It's hard writing this, because sometimes that's a road I walk, but you have to want it as much as the air you need to breathe. In short, there is no other way. If you aren't willing to put the work in, if you aren't willing to make sacrifices, then you will never, ever make it to the top of your game.

Aim For The Stars

This book isn't about becoming a millionaire. It's about the journey to whatever target you set yourself, and the challenges you face in getting there. I want to give you the tools to take on anything that stands in the way of achieving your dream. With the right mindset, purpose, positivity and passion, you can aim for the stars. What matters is that you don't feel held back as that goal comes into focus.

Thinking big in this way isn't always about wealth, of course. It might not even be about your business, but your family or mental health. We're talking about ambitions here, and numbers may not come into it. Money can bring some happiness, in the form of peace of mind, but it can also cause a great deal of grief. Creative goals, on the other hand, can give rise to a sense of fulfilment that's as valid as a pay cheque, if not more. It brings with it the chance to make a mark on life, leave a stamp or legacy. Ambition is such a personal thing, but all of us owe it to ourselves to be fearless in identifying our goals. We must be unafraid to be bold.

With the Haye/Harrison fight behind me, and a stable of exciting boxers who were looking to me to fulfil their career potential, I took some time in 2012 to assess the state of the sport. It struck me that all the shows that made it onto television in this country were staged in leisure centres or civic halls. The ring itself would often be set up on an indoor basketball court, and so the floor markings made it look like it didn't belong.

Then there was the seating, which was usually half empty, because frankly who wants to spend money on a night out at a place where you normally take the kids to sports clubs? All those folded rows looked terrible on the screen, and drew your attention to the fact that you could see a car park in the drizzle outside. Even if the fight itself was watchable, there was no atmosphere, no excitement, and no future.

Through my eyes, as someone passionate about the sport, boxing was dying. It was all about the perception, really, because what went on inside the ropes could be compelling. In the hands of people who appeared to have lost interest, however, there was no hope that it could appeal beyond a shrinking hard core of fans. At the same time, I had a vision. It was fearless, big and bold, because I believed that boxing deserved to be up there with the Premiership and Formula 1.

People might have dismissed my ambition as a fantasy, something way beyond my reach, but I knew I had the passion, positivity, drive and mindset to make it happen. These were my raw materials. I wasn't interested in giving a shine to the shows we were expected to watch on our TV screens. I wanted to restart boxing on a scale that befitted the sport.

Unafraid to put in the work and make the sacrifices, I rolled up my sleeves and started building from scratch.

'I want to take over British boxing,' I told my dad, when I was ready to share my proposal. 'All of it.'

Dad looked at me to check he had heard me right.

'My advice is to steer clear of boxing altogether,' he said. 'It's the worst business in the world.'

I knew he'd respond in this way before slowly coming round to back me, but he needed a moment to get up to speed with my direction of travel. To help him through the gears, I laid out my reasoning. In its current form, with the same promoters carving up the shows available for broadcast on Sky, things had become complacent. Dad recognised that, and didn't disagree. Nobody was fighting for the right to stage the fights, and that included my old man. As much as he loved boxing, he viewed the sport as finished.

Now I was standing before him with absolute bags of ambition, purpose and passion. Boxing is all about narrative. Always had been, and still could be in the right hands. We need the big fights, I told him, the arenas, the anticipation and the electric atmosphere that used to make those shows so explosive.

'We have to create the perception,' I said to finish, 'that the sport is a *monster*.'

As I saw things, going in big was the only way forward. All the barriers my dad put up motivated me even more, and confirmed in my mind that scale was key in this sport. To be successful in any business, you have to possess enough confidence in your product and yourself to know that it's an unbeatable combination. In this case, that meant blowing the competition out of the water to create the space to deliver my vision.

I also knew that in executing my plan, I would be taking things much further than my dad ever did. It wasn't a question of trying to outperform him. In a way, I wanted to do this because in the end he'd walked away from a sport he loved. Why? Because there was never much love lost between the promoters on the scene. When boxing began to lose its appeal as I was growing up, and ticket sales dwindled with viewing figures, it became more challenging for them all to make it properly profitable. The increased stress and strains that came with it meant the promoters were often banging heads together. Eventually, my dad had enough.

'Do you know what?' he said at the time. 'I'm going to do the darts. There's less aggro, less hassle and more money. The players can't believe they've been given this chance, unlike the boxers. They say hello in the morning, please and thank you, Eddie. It's just a better business.'

It was the right move for my dad at the time, but brought with it the suggestion that he'd been driven out of the game by the other promoters. That stayed with me a bit, as did those memories of lying on his study floor as a kid. Often, back then, Dad was fighting battles with those guys, as well as the big American promoters. Emotions could heat up, and sometimes that escalated into screaming and shouting. You register that kind of thing when you're younger, along with the fact that it would often leave my old man exasperated.

So, as I developed my plan to go big with boxing, there was a part of me that wanted to fight some of those battles for my dad. None of this was personal and I had no beef with the promoters I'd have to take on. I'd escaped that cloud of negativity long ago. I also didn't know them like Dad did. They simply stood between me and my goal to revitalise boxing. Any of them would've been welcome to raise their game to meet me – that's healthy competition, which was lacking in the sport. In my bones, however, with the vision I planned to deliver and the energy and drive I provided, I knew that I could win.

If you're going to be successful, you have to be confident in your own abilities and who you are. If you're already leading a company or just starting out, being confident in the workplace and having a strong sense of self-belief is crucial. You'll present yourself better, communicate ideas more clearly, and you'll make better decisions when it comes to your career. You'll know what you want and how to achieve it. This mindset can only have a positive impact on you, and those around you.

Dare to Succeed

Growing up, I watched my dad taking massive risks in business. By his own admission, he was reckless. He can say that now, looking back at his career, because despite some of the losses he picked up along the way, he has consolidated his successes. Age has encouraged caution, and why not? He achieved his dreams and doesn't want to lose the life it's earned him.

I was only starting on my journey. Like anyone in my position, with an ambition to take things even further, the temptation was to gamble with my future. Why would anyone put in the long slog to achieve a dream, when they can throw the dice and hope it'll take them there quicker? My answer was to flag up the fact that fate might not look kindly upon me, as my dad discovered to his cost a couple of times. I remembered the scrape he had when a snooker sponsor went bust, and had only to remind myself of the close shave I'd experienced when I considered accepting a poker stake through a gaming account.

Being aware that risk can be dangerous doesn't mean you have to be averse to it. If I was someone who ran scared of risk, and the possibility it brings of failure, I'd have played it safe and looked after Matchroom's share of the fights divvied up among the same promoters. It also wouldn't have got me anywhere. I would probably have achieved a gradual growth, along with people saying, 'Well, you couldn't really fail, could you? You had the company.' And they'd have been right.

If I was going to outstrip my dad's achievements, then I needed to factor risk into the equation. My responsibility to the business – and the same goes for anyone pursuing a bold ambition – was to devise a strategy along with meticulous financial planning to turn this from a blag into a solid power move.

In my view, risk is something that can be managed, minimised or even eradicated with careful consideration. There is a huge difference, I think, between being reckless with your business and being daring. In the pursuit of success, I am a big believer in the latter. I dared to be bigger and better than all the other boxing promoters, but the plan I had in place wasn't thrown hastily together in a bid to strike lucky. I examined every aspect, and welcomed my dad's doubts and misgivings, because that gave me a chance to test it first.

Every time I considered what could hurt me unless I was ready, I came away with my conviction reinforced that I could do this. Having reviewed every detail of my plan, the risks I ran were covered off.

But the dare that underpinned it was incredible. I had a plan to overturn the system and every day the hunger grew.

With my small team of big boxers signed to me, I arranged a meeting with Barney Francis, who was managing director of Sky Sports. Matchroom had been Sky partners for decades but Barney had been in the hot seat around a year at this point. Like my dad, I'm a great believer in straight talking. It cuts out time-wasting, everyone can see the cards on the table and make an informed decision.

'I want all the dates,' I said. 'Give me the boxing and I'll show you what can be done with it.'

'We can't do that,' said Barney, which came as no surprise, before he reminded me that Sky had five months left on its contracts with Warren, Maloney and Hatton, as well as Matchroom. The Friday fights were divided up fairly between the promoters, which kept everyone happy, and that's how it was.

'Yeah, but nobody is working with each other,' I said. 'Nobody is *trying* or pushing the boundaries, and the viewers are switching off. We need to bring back that Saturday night buzz. It's not there any more.'

Despite the opinion upstairs that boxing was dead, Barney shared our vision that we needed to bring boxing back on Saturday nights and he always believed in the sport. There were two things I knew about Barney: he liked boxing and he was a straight-shooter. If I had a chance to show him that the sport could be revitalised, I figured I might have an ally. With less than half a year to go before the contracts were up for renewal, I knew what time I had left to win him over.

'Barney,' I said before leaving. 'I'm going to show you what can be done.'

It was a good meeting, in that it gave me a chance to make my intentions known. There was no way that Sky were simply going to take my word for it. I was well aware of that. All I asked was that he remember this conversation, because I guaranteed that he would look back and know that I was the future of British boxing.

As an opening round, it was bold and ballsy. Barney Francis wasn't going to forget some new promoter breezing in like this and I knew he wouldn't forget the plan. In effect, I'd set out my stall. No hints. No teasing. This is what I can do. The next step in my strategy was to demonstrate that I had the ability to turn a blue-sky dream for boxing into reality.

It was in this meeting that I learned that you have to take opportunities when they come your way. When you're presented with an opportunity, you can't be afraid to go after it because you might not get another one. You have to learn to back yourself 100 per cent because you're the only one who's going to make it happen. Nobody else is going to do it for you. I've learned that in business there are times when you have to take the risk, otherwise you lose the opportunity. You have to be prepared to throw it all on the line and put yourself out there because, ultimately, that's when things will start to happen.

Strategic Thinking

Achieving your goals and being successful requires hard work and focus. Things aren't going to be given to you just because you want them. You can't expect to stand in one place and then be taken to the next. In 2014, I ran the London Marathon. It was one of the hardest things I've ever done, and I earned that medal. Like anyone who's ever stood on that starting line for the first time, the finish is so far away, and it's all down to you to reach the end. Running just over twenty-six miles is hard to get your head around, and all manner of doubts can creep in before the gun has even gone off. It's easy to start overthinking the whole thing. That's when it can all go wrong before you've even begun, and the same applies to business.

I came away from that meeting with Sky having made a large-scale statement of intent. It would've been easy to have headed back to the Matchroom offices and panicked, but I didn't.

If you're going in big with your ambitions, that destination can seem so far away it's impossible to reach. It means the only way forward is to break down the journey into realistic steps. That way, every day you reach the promised land before moving onto the next one. Call it a roadmap, a list of tasks to tick off that will take you there, or a strategy. Whatever method you choose to divide things up, there's only one thing that matters: you have to stick to it, and keep building on the momentum.

My dad is a seasoned marathon runner. He's taken part in quite a few big city events, with a seriously decent personal best time of 3 hours 19 minutes. On his first ever attempt, he came in at just under 4 hours. Dad being who he is, he spent years telling me that I didn't have it in me to go the distance. So, what choice did I have?

When I received confirmation that I had a place, I gave it to my dad as a Christmas present. His face lit up. He couldn't believe it, and was so happy that I'd taken up the challenge. All I wanted to do was get under 4 hours and beat his first marathon time. Nothing else mattered to me. I trained my nuts off so I was in good shape, and when the big day came I felt ready.

The first few miles went well. The atmosphere as a runner in the London Marathon is incredible and I was looking forward to seeing my family at the end. Not least my dad when I beat his first time. Towards the halfway mark, however, my legs began to feel heavy. From there on out, the thought of seeing my old man, my wife and kids at the finish line seemed to shrink into the distance.

All I could do was plug away, one mile at a time, and get the job done. There was no alternative to achieve what I set out to do, which was complete one fucking marathon. By eighteen miles, which is when most people hit the wall, my focus went no further than passing one landmark and then the next. It was the only way that I could progress, until finally I faced the last few miles and the end was literally in sight.

I missed out on beating my dad's first time by only a few minutes, but that didn't matter. Anyone who completes a marathon for the first time knows what a massive undertaking it is. The sense of achievement is incredible. What I hadn't realised, until I stood there with a medal around my neck, is the similarities with life and business.

Ultimately, the only way to take on that distance, which can seem impossible if you think too far ahead, is to run it one mile at a time. In the same way, no matter how ambitious the undertaking before you, break it down into manageable sections and you can achieve the impossible.

It all comes down to strategy. It's about forward planning, and considering all the nuts and bolts you'll have to take care of along the way. You can have a long-term plan that turns your goal into a stepping stone to something bigger, but first you have to reach that goal before you can take things further. Otherwise you'll get halfway and give up. I'm a big believer in taking care of mental health, and this is an effective means of managing stress and pressure, as well as staying strong and on track.

Boxers employ the same strategy. If they're in their corner facing their opponent, they can't be thinking twelve rounds ahead. The nervous energy would burn them out before the first bell. Crucially, for me, the only way to go the distance in business is by setting out my short-term strategies. Keep it regimented, straightforward and simple. Ask yourself what you have to do to reach that next mile marker and then get it done.

With the outcome of the Sky Sports meeting in my mind, I sat down and assembled a plan. I fully intended to take control of British boxing. That was my finish line before I could move onto anything else, and the promise I had made to Barney. I had been quite prepared to be laughed out of town. That would've been fine – what mattered was that I had made him aware of my ambitions. Next I figured out all the markers I would need to pass in order to demonstrate that we were number one in the game. Here, I was looking at the landscape ahead and working out the relationships I'd need to make. Everything I listed shared the same objective: to get me over that line.

Naturally I shared the next stage of my plan with my old man.

'I'm going to put on a fight between Kell Brook and Matthew Hatton,' I said. Kell was my recent signing, and Matthew was Ricky Hatton's brother. In my view, this was a fight that could produce fireworks. Not only that, with Kell hailing from Yorkshire and going up against Lancashire-born Matthew, there was only one way we could sell it. 'We're going to call it the War of the Roses,' I went on, 'and we're going to stage it at Sheffield Arena.'

'Arena shows are finished,' my dad said. 'They're too expensive. We don't even sell out leisure centres nowadays.'

'That's because the shows aren't worth watching,' I came back at him. 'This is the only way to make boxing unmissable. I have to make it a big event.'

'Son, Sheffield Arena holds eight thousand people.'

'I will sell out,' I promised.

Dad considered me for a moment. I wasn't backing down. I was absolutely convinced that this stood as a vital first step in the strategy.

'Just do it properly,' my dad said eventually, and I knew I had his backing. 'That means paying your fighters the right amount. Don't mess them around.'

'I've already done the figures,' I said. 'I'm going to offer them one hundred grand each.'

'Are you mad?'

Dad nearly choked in disbelief. He's always been a great believer in honesty when it comes to negotiations, but in his opinion, these figures didn't match the return he anticipated.

'I've done the figures,' I assured him. 'We sell out the arena and it works.'

'But you got to sell out the arena, Eddie. That's easier said than done!'

I asked him to trust me, and I took the offer to the fighters in turn. By any standard, for this level of boxing, it was a lot of money. I wanted to demonstrate that I believed in this clash, and wanted both Brook and Hatton to be as committed as me. By now, I was sold on my own event. Nobody had forgotten the Haye/Harrison fight, but people remembered the spectacle more than the performance in the ring. I planned to build on all the elements of the show that had made that fight a success for the War of the Roses. I wanted the lights, music and celebrities.

With a single-minded focus, I worked to create the excitement that I remembered feeling as a kid watching fights. When Naseem Hamed came out on a flying carpet? That blew my mind, and I wanted to do the same thing again in terms of pure spectacle.

The upshot? In front of a sell-out crowd, Kell Brook secured a convincing victory. The fight went the distance, and the event was deemed a massive success. Most importantly, as I started thinking about the next step in my plan, Sky enjoyed ratings that were four times what they expected for a normal Saturday fight night. Barney Francis couldn't be anything other than impressed, and I reinforced what was required to deliver boxing at this scale every time.

With contracts still to run between Sky and the other promoters, I wasn't surprised that I would need to pass another few markers before my finish line came within sight. It was something I'd built into the plan. I couldn't afford to come across as impatient and piss him off. This was the guy negotiating Premier League rights, and now he had some oik who wanted to bring back boxing by trying to take control.

I also knew how to apply pressure in the right way.

At this point, the fans had begun to pick up on the fact that this young guy had come in to deliver fights worth watching, and they were getting behind me. I started using social media to build that relationship, and stoke enthusiasm for future fights or boxers I had signed.

While other rivals were still posting up flyers on underpasses, I would go on Twitter and reach out directly to a massive audience on their phones. It was the perfect medium to build hype, knowing I could deliver. I also used it indirectly to remind the only nationwide broadcaster then doing boxing that dream fights could be possible if only we had sole control.

For the fans, I represented a breath of fresh air. I was young, loud and passionate about the sport. I made people laugh, sometimes with me and occasionally at my expense, but that was fine, because I sensed they wanted me to stage the big fights I promised. I was a promoter intent on supercharging the sport, not grasping it as a nice little earner.

Carl Froch was a mandatory challenger for Lucian Bute's IBF super-middleweight belt and the fight would go on to be one of the most exciting fights I have ever had the honour to put together. We staged it at the Capital FM Arena in Nottingham, called it 'No Easy Way Out', and invested the same commitment to scale and ambition as my previous shows. Froch was very much the underdog, but with the home crowd behind him, he came through in five electric rounds to bust up Bute big time and stop him on his feet.

It was magnificent. Not only one of the best nights in British boxing, but a viewing sensation on Sky. I was so delighted for Froch that I crashed through the ropes to bear hug him from behind before the referee had finished counting out Bute. I felt like such a tit when I realised, and a little panic-stricken in case I'd invalidated the fight, but fortunately the referee hadn't noticed. And when he did signal it was all over, the arena erupted.

The next time I saw Barney, he had only one thing to say to me.

'I'll back you.'

When I first told my dad I wanted to seize control of boxing in the UK, I wasn't joking. I had identified my goal and then set up a series of markers in order to achieve it. With the exclusive deal from Sky, and all the old promoters cut loose, I was able to go to other boxers and show them how their careers could grow by joining my stable. I offered ambition, excitement, commitment and drive. There would be no more complacency, no cosy carve-up of the fights, because I had plans for the sport that were game-changing.

Even before the ink on the deal had dried, the Sky takeover was no longer my finish line in boxing. As a strategy, it was a vital first step on a journey to the world stage.

And a young fighter called Anthony Joshua was set to come with me.

Investing in the Future

With a solid business strategy, you can grow stronger with every step. The finish line might still seem out of reach, but slowly you're consolidating on successes and building the momentum.

With the Sky deal in place, I became the promoter who trainers' approached with fighters who showed potential. I had to pick carefully, of course. My reputation could only be as good as my stable, after all. One time, I received a letter out of nowhere from a boxing club representative. It was an odd request for help. This club had a promising heavyweight fighter by the name of Anthony Joshua. According to the letter, young Anthony was in a little trouble with the law, having been caught with cannabis. The guy writing to me explained that Anthony had a promising career ahead of him that could be derailed by the case, and asked if I could testify for him in court.

I read the letter in full, thinking, *Are you having a laugh? I don't even know this kid*, and binned it.

But I remembered the name.

A few months later, I was in Sheffield to see Carl Froch. He trained in the boxing gym at the English Institute of Sport under the watchful eye of Rob McCracken. Now, Rob is one of the finest coaches out there, so as well as catching up with Froch, it was good to get Rob's opinion on fighters to watch. That day, we hadn't even had that conversation when I heard this deep, rhythmic creaking coming from another room. I recognised it as the noise made by a chain supporting a heavy bag from a concrete pillar. It's not an unusual sound to hear in a gym, but this was intense

'Who's in there?' I asked Rob, who grinned at me.

'That's AJ,' he said. 'He can *fight*.'

I tried to think of any fighters with a name that matched those initials, and the penny dropped.

'Didn't he have a court case recently?' I asked.

'All sorted,' said Rob. 'He's just been selected to represent Team GB in the Olympics.'

So, kicking myself for not answering his club's appeal for help, I popped my head around the door to watch this young guy working out. I had only to look at the expression of sheer concentration on Anthony's face to know that combined with his power and technique, he was going places. As a promoter, however, I only represented boxers when they turned professional. With the Olympics imminent, all I could think was that I hoped he didn't win. Then it could get messy if he turned pro – with other promoters also trying to sign him – and expensive.

The 2012 Olympics were staged in London. The whole nation got behind Team GB, and Anthony became a national hero when he won gold. I was delighted for him, and a little bit gutted. I called Rob to congratulate him, and ask if he'd put in a word.

'AJ is his own man,' said Rob. 'I'm sure he'll talk to you when he's ready.'

So, now it was me left hanging, hoping he would respond, and to AJ's credit he did just that.

When we met, I wasn't struck so much by his formidable size as his intellect. He had so many questions for me about how I did business, which I respected hugely. Eventually, keen to do the right thing, I suggested he go away and see as many promoters as he could. Then, having grilled them in the same way, he could make an informed decision.

AJ agreed to do that and I thought, *Fuck, I hope he comes back*.

It took him six months, but this is one conscientious guy. With his Olympic gold still gleaming, AJ had the pick of the promoters, and he chose to come with me. Why? Anthony will tell you it's because he liked the family business and I was significantly younger than all the other promoters, plus he recognised I had the passion to do something truly special with his career. He made his own decision, but on that last note I knew it was the right one.

I was still focusing on one marker after another, pursuing my dream, but it was quite clear to me that AJ would play a part in making that come true. We could help each other. AJ was a serious talent in the ring, while I could offer the same thing outside it. We shared the same positivity, drive and mindset, and the unflinching belief that with hard work and commitment true greatness was within reach.

In building AJ's career, he really did prove to be an unstoppable force, and living proof that hard work always pays off. His early victories in the ring with Matchroom were nothing less than decisive, and we kept up the momentum in terms of fights as he won both the Commonwealth and British titles. We took AJ from the O2 Arena to the Manchester Arena, and continued to scale up our ambitions with every marker passed. It wasn't only about numbers in terms of viewers and fans, or size when it came to venues. AJ is such a powerhouse that watching him box is always history in the making.

Like me, Anthony knew that there was no way he could be the best version of himself without putting in the work others refused to do.

That doesn't just apply to boxing. It cuts across all forms of business. Hard work is what will set you apart from the others. When you're willing to put the extra effort in, you will achieve your goals. If you're not prepared to put in 100 per cent, then you won't be the best person you can be. Put in 50 per cent and that's what you'll get, but neither of us do anything by half.

ROUND 5 – KEY TAKEAWAYS

- One thing that is important for me to tell you is that 'thinking big' is not always about your bottom line. Making money is great and, sure, it can bring some kind of happiness, but the ability to overcome obstacles and reach goals is so much more rewarding. That sense of achievement and fulfilment is always the feeling that gives me the most happiness; it's a money-can't-buy moment. At times I've felt as much satisfaction from a fighter winning a southern area title as I have a fighter unifying world titles. It's those little moments that make you feel on top of the world.

- You may hear it a lot in this book, but I cannot stress the importance of taking care of your short-term goals. I'm a believer in planning for the future, of course, but there are too many dreamers in this world who are not willing to tick the boxes to get their fantasies off the ground. So take care of the fundamentals, get the bread and butter done, and only then will the bigger picture start to unfold.

- How many times have you started something and failed to finish? Well, for me, it's dozens of times. But on which of those occasions did you feel any sense of achievement or fulfilment? Life is a game of survival; get your nut down, crack on and take care of business from start to finish.

Round 6

PREPARATION FOR LIFE

If I had to count all the skills needed to stage a show successfully, I'd quickly run out of fingers. It's not a job that requires formal training. There is no Academy for Boxing Promoters. From securing deals and fine-tuning contracts, to hosting press conferences and talking fighters who've lost a belt into believing they can still triumph, pretty much everything I do is the sum total of my experience in life so far.

I just didn't know it at the time.

What we're talking about here is awareness. Every day of our lives, we're learning. With a mindset focused on achieving, we're also getting stronger. Experience is such a *valuable* asset, no matter what your business ambition. It can provide you with the confidence, knowledge and skills required to work to the best of your ability, and the wisdom to keep it clear and simple at all times. That way, it doesn't matter how grand your vision, or how many balls you have to keep up in the air, ultimately you can say with absolute conviction that you will get it done.

Learning from Experience

Whatever goal you've set for yourself, even if it demands some kind of training, you're still going to rely on skills from the school of life. A professional poker player has to learn the rules of the game before starting out, but nobody can teach them to stay cool with a weak hand at a World Series event and then set about taking down their opponents. Whether it's an ability to keep your nerve under pressure, or pick yourself up from rejection and come back stronger, it all stems from moments in life we call character-building.

The first time we experience such a thing, often learning something the hard way, it doesn't come with a certificate to say we can now handle the same event in future. If anything, as we face test after test in pursuing success, we have a growing awareness that we've faced a similar situation before. That gives us something to build on. A muscle memory we can flex on demand. In some cases, it's a question of repetition. If you find yourself in the same situation again and again, then eventually it becomes easier. But it's only with the right mindset to succeed that it becomes second nature.

The first time I faced a pre-fight press conference, I was sweating buckets. I had to fight hard to keep my nerves from showing. I was looking into camera lenses, expected to perform, and had to fight to pull it off. I was still bricking it for the second press conference, but somehow it didn't seem as bad. Fast forward a few shows, and I could address the media feeling more like myself. Cut to today, and I can stand at the dais for a World Title fight, facing the glare of the media, and my heart won't miss a beat. I've done it so many times that I'm familiar with the process, thoughts and feelings involved.

I can do a press conference with my eyes shut, but I'm not asleep at the wheel. Far from it. Familiarity can lead to complacency, and yet my passion for boxing is so intense that when I stand in front of the microphone, I can't wait to start talking. Steve Davis once offered me words of wisdom, which to be fair is part of his job role as my godfather. He said that he no longer feels any sense of anxiety when playing snooker in front of an audience, because 'the nerve endings have disintegrated', and I know what he means. The more you do something the easier it gets, and if it's a regular feature on your road to success, then it frees you up to get *better* at it every time. Ultimately, you've got to love what you do.

Then there are the transferable skills that come from certain experiences and situations. We never go into them thinking they will help us in future, but on a subconscious level, it's a learning process. Often the episodes that stay with us, and teach us the most, are those that drag us from our comfort zones.

One of my childhood boxing heroes was a fighter called Paul 'Silky' Jones. I was in awe of his dedication, grit and determination, as well as him being a thoroughly nice guy. My dad often took me with him so I could watch Silky fight, and the boxer would even let me carry his belts out to the ring beforehand.

One time we travelled to Northern Ireland to watch him take on Damien Denny for the WBO Intercontinental Super Welterweight Title. The fight was at the Ulster Hall, which is a brilliant old building with balcony seating. Being a hometown boy, Denny had massive support behind him. The build-up was incredible, but through my eyes Silky was a superhero who could not be beaten.

Before the fight, with the crowds in the hall chanting Denny's name, I was in the changing room as Silky made his final preparations. He was focused, in the zone and listening to his coach. Then, out of nowhere, this boxer who was carved from stone evaporated. One moment Silky was calm and collected, the next he seemed to be having a complete breakdown.

I froze, unable to take my eyes off him. I remember one of his team coming over and steering me away, but that moment shocked me to the core.

From a boxing point of view, it looked like his head had gone. As far as I was concerned, he'd lost the fight before the first bell. It was a surprise to see Silky looking fine as he made his ring walk. I figured the confidence had to be a front to hide the fact that he was broken.

That night, it took Silky only one round to win the title. Denny did not stand a chance against such powerful, venomous punches, and he was counted out flat on his back.

Back in the dressing room, when I finally got a chance to slip in, Silky and his team were celebrating hard. I even had a chance to congratulate him, and being a kid with no developed sense of tact, I asked him outright what happened in the changing room.

'I just wanted the win so bad, Ed,' he told me. 'I'd trained so hard for this opportunity, and suddenly it had arrived.'

Decades later, as I approached the finish of the London Marathon, I remembered that night and realised exactly what Silky had meant. The path to success is long and challenging. When you want to achieve your goals, you must be willing to give everything to make it happen. It comes down to the realisation that you have made sacrifices to reach this point and now it's about to pay off.

Thanks to Silky, when I'm with a boxer in the final moments before a ring walk, I know what's going through their mind. I don't even have to say anything. If they don't allow their emotion to come through, I'm better prepared to do my job by being aware that it's there under the surface.

There are countless moments in our lives, starting from a very early age, that make us who we are today. You have to remember these when things get tough. I witnessed so many formative episodes as a kid, accompanying my old man to fights, that it was almost like a schooling to become a boxing promoter. I remember catching my breath at the Royal Albert Hall when another one of my heroes Jim McDonnell took a punch and got knocked out clean. I was sitting in the front row, and Jimmy cracked down on the bottom rope with his eyes wide open. In those days, there were fewer medics on hand. Jim lay there, motionless on his back, until his team rushed a stretcher through the crowd and he was taken to the changing room and placed on a table until he woke.

You don't forget things like that in your early years, and I'm glad to say that Jim came round in the dressing room. As a promoter, I've seen it happen several times since, but that memory helps me to focus on what needs to be done. As a result, I don't freeze and hope someone else knows the procedure to get that fighter medical attention. I'm on it, because I've seen it all before.

The way I see things, everything in our past can contribute to success as we move on. Nothing should be written off or considered useless. Both good and bad events can stand you in good stead in other ways at some point in the future. When I dialled the first number in the phone book at Weatherseal, and got told to fuck off, I didn't think my instinct to ring that number again would seed the mindset I needed to never stop getting the deal done.

There really is nothing more difficult than cold calling. It's unquestionably the most challenging thing to do in any business, and when you're trying to flog windows, that's the lowest of the low. The rejection is off the scale. It *destroys* the soul. As a grounding in resilience and thinking on my feet, however, that experience was priceless. It showed me rejection time and time again but taught me a great deal about myself and the value of determination and drive.

With the right mindset, those ups, downs, trials and tests that you will definitely go through can be drawn upon to help you achieve. If you want to get through the hard times, the rough patches, you need to be able to face a challenge head on. This is where drive and determination have to come in. Your dedication to making something happen will set you apart from the others. Success comes to those who are determined not to fail and have the drive to keep going when things go wrong.

Fail to Prepare, Prepare to Fail

As I've mentioned before, your experiences in life shape who you are. They affect everything from your values to your skillset. Equally important, however, is preparation. Being prepared is an essential skill that will get you ahead in business and one that you need to be successful. It's a question of asking yourself what needs to be done before you take on a task, so you can execute it to the best of your abilities.

In some areas, my attention to preparation can be quite front end. I'm notorious in the office for sometimes coming up with an idea and then creating space for my team to figure out how to get it off the ground while I move onto the next one. It's a conscious decision that works for Matchroom, because it frees up my energies to keep pushing our ambitions, knowing I have people I trust with my life to deliver. Personally, I prefer to keep it loose and trust my instincts. It's the seller in me, I suppose; ready to push on and react to whatever barriers land in the way of a deal.

Obviously, there is a big difference between floating new ideas and preparing for a show, but the fundamentals remain the same. It's vital that I know exactly what's going on at any moment when preparing for a show. I lay out everything that needs to be done and then I'm on it. It demands discipline and commitment to see it through, but I'm lucky enough to be working in a sport where the competitors are an example.

When we watch a boxer climbing through the ropes, they've arrived at the end of a long journey. It's been months in the making, living a regimented lifestyle that puts preparation at the forefront of everything they do. People say I work hard, but these guys are up at 5.30 a.m. every morning, come rain or shine. They'll knock out a ten-mile run before anyone else is up and go back to bed for a short rest, before sparring for ten rounds. Back home they'll rest and eat, before moving onto strength and conditioning work. They're in bed by eleven, no matter what, and then rinse and repeat as they plug through a training programme that eventually brings them under the spotlight in a packed-out arena.

At that moment, all the preparation is over. They are ready, physically and mentally, so that whatever happens when the bell for round one rings, they can say they did everything they could.

These men and women are an example to me. The sacrifices they make are incredible, from strict weight management to missing out on moments at home they might never get back again. But they do it because they're dedicated to the pursuit of victory. They have to be able to look at their own reflection and say with absolute conviction that they were fully prepared for the battle.

The way I see it, if you're working towards a goal and determined it's going to be a success, then you need to ask yourself the same thing: have I done everything in my power to make this happen?

Simplicity and Success

My dad taught me to be a straight-talker. In his view, it's the most efficient and effective way to get things done, and he's right. Even to this day, he reminds me not to overcomplicate things or create problems for myself by being too clever.

When I went to him with plans to stage that arena fight between Brook and Hatton, I explained that based on my projected sales, we had a budget to pay each fighter one hundred thousand pounds. The purses were nothing compared to what they are today, but it was a massive amount back then. I wanted to guarantee that I had them both, because the pairing was solid.

'I thought I'd start at seventy-five grand,' I said to Dad, 'and then negotiate from there.'

'What's the point?' he said. 'You've just told me what you can pay.'

'Well, they might settle for less than a hundred,' I said, thinking of the money we'd save.

Dad looked at me as if I needed to have a long, hard think about this.

'Why fuck about?' he asked. 'If you want this fight to happen, save yourself time by just getting in there and getting it done.'

So, with that advice in mind, I went to Matthew Hatton first. I didn't think he wanted to fight that badly. When I made him the offer, the full 100K, I knew his eyes would pop out of his head. I was also ready for his next question, which to be fair, any other boxer would've asked.

'Is there any more?'

'Not a penny,' I said, with such absolute honesty, he could read it in me.

I applied the approach to Kell Brook – laid it out to him straight. In each case, with both fighters knowing they were being treated fairly and transparently, we signed the contract there and then.

When you do a deal like this, with no pulling punches, it makes business run smoothly. It means if you're working towards a greater goal, like an arena fight in my case, then there's no risk of it coming back to bite. In being fair to both boxers, I could expect to be treated with the same honesty and respect. They were paid properly, because I recognised their worth, and that bought energy and commitment from them.

If a fighter ever feels that I've fucked them, then I'll pay for it at some point. They might show up late for the press conference, or be difficult with me throughout the whole process. The fact is I had a budget. Yes, I could've struck a hard bargain, and saved myself a few quid, but it would have cost me in ways I'd rather avoid.

Instead I kept it very simple, and very fair, and both fighters delivered a great fight.

In working towards success, there's a lot to be said for simplicity. Your goal might involve many moving parts. If so, strip down each component to serve its intended function. Don't try to be clever if it risks slowing the momentum you're building to get the job done.

In April 2017, Anthony Joshua defended his IBF title, and challenged for the WBA (super) and IBO (heavyweight) titles, against Wladimir Klitschko. We staged the fight at Wembley Stadium in front of 90,000 fans, an unheard-of figure, who witnessed one of Joshua's greatest victories after eleven brutal and spellbinding rounds. What people didn't see, in the stadium or watching on the edge of their seats at home, was all the preparation that my team and I put into it.

There were so many markers between the concept for a fight on this scale and the reality. At any one time, I had countless challenges to overcome, any one of which could have scuppered the whole event. Firstly, there's all the time-consuming tasks that have to be tackled in staging any boxing show, from contract negotiations to dealing with competing broadcasters, ticket pricing, and then driving sales including pay-per-view. But with a venue of this size, and the sheer volume of fans, the logistics covering transport, health and safety proved endless.

I must give credit to the Mayor of London, Sadiq Khan, for his support and cooperation as we worked through all the issues. He had my back, and not only because of his belief that the discipline and purpose boxing offers can change young lives for the better.

For all the support, however, and a team that worked night and day on making that fight happen, I had to keep it simple. With so many moving parts, it was the only way to keep the juggernaut rolling. The demands we faced were intense, but by keeping the complications to a minimum we got it done. It was about smart thinking without trying to be clever, and being transparent as a means of doing business. I aim to build trust and cooperation, because working together with people instead of against them brings you closer to your goal.

Simplicity doesn't make things easy, of course. In the same

way, being up front with people can be the harder option. It's just that both are solid strategies when it comes to delivering on a project that your competitors wouldn't touch because it seemed impossible at the outset. That's what excites me in some ways. All my peers had been content with staging shows in pony sports halls, and even those places were often half empty. I went to Wembley Stadium, driven by passion and the belief that I could create one of the best nights of boxing this country's ever had.

No matter how much preparation and sacrifice that demanded, I had to do it. Saying it couldn't be done was for other people. I wanted it too badly. With momentum on my side, and pure positivity, I had to work through all the processes in turn, with the mindset to say I will get there in the end.

I love the saying: pressure creates diamonds. That's exactly what came into existence on that night in the eleventh round. Both boxers had fought like lions throughout, but this was the moment AJ imposed his dominance and the referee called it. The fans and the viewing public witnessed a spectacular fight with a dream outcome. For Anthony, my team and me, that fight was the last mile in that marathon, where everything had to go to plan in order to make it such a success.

The victory was stunning, the scale of the show out of this world, but the simplicity behind every stage of the preparation process lay at the heart of it all.

Preparation is a skill that you can learn and, with discipline and experience, can improve and develop over time. It might not come naturally to you, but it plays an important role in your development. Once you have it nailed down, you'll be able to react quicker and be more efficient when things go wrong.

Do Not Be Outworked

Whatever I set out to achieve in business, I won't sleep at night unless I know that I have worked harder than anybody else. The only way to do that, and be sure that every thought and moment counts that you put into the process, is to be passionate about what you do. Without it, there is no way that you'll have the gas in the tank and what it takes to outperform your competitors.

There is no alternative. You cannot make sacrifices for the sake of a goal unless the unconditional drive behind it is in your bones. It's possible to achieve something without really caring about it, but greatness won't come into it. That has to come from the heart. You have to live and love the business so it consumes your life. It keeps that fire going inside of you and keeps the drive going. Others will see your enthusiasm and passion, and this can have a positive effect on your team.

The sense of relentlessness that you need to be successful isn't something you can summon at will. Few wake up in the morning, facing some task that doesn't excite them, with fire in their belly. That has to come from within. It's about being massively passionate about your aims and objectives.

Look at Bob Arum, a legendary American promoter who has been inducted into the Boxing Hall of Fame. Bob is in his eighties. He's been championing boxing for sixty years now, and still goes to every show. He's an old guy, frail around the edges, but brimming with dedication and enthusiasm for what he does. Listen to him talk about a fight and he comes alive. This is a man who has never been outworked in his life. He has put in more graft than any of his competitors (until me!), which is one more demand on the path to longevity and greatness.

Of course, you can be the most fired-up business player in the world, committed to what you're doing, and still have a bad day. There are times when I look at a schedule of media interviews I'm expected to do, and my first thought is that I have a whole list of other things I could be doing. It's a fleeting thing, because then I remind myself that I have a responsibility to handle the press to the best of my abilities, if the business or show is going to be truly successful.

You won't love what you do every day, but you will do if you lose it. That's why you have to select what you do so wisely. How many people are in 9-to-5 jobs that they loathe? If it suits you, that's great. You get your money, you go home and forget all about work. The weekdays are a grind, but the weekends are all yours. You can switch off, and I'm often envious of that. At the same time, I feel a little sad for those who feel trapped by this kind of existence, or who don't have the courage to pursue their dreams. Each to their own, but personally I don't stop thinking about work from the moment I wake up to the second I go to sleep.

All successful people have an underlying passion for what they do. If you are unhappy in your job, or completely stressed out, that negativity is going to affect how others see you. But if you have a clear drive to succeed, and you approach your work with enthusiasm, it won't go unnoticed. Work has to consume every aspect of your life, but not only that, you have to allow the work to take over every aspect of your existence. You can't resent it, or try to escape from it, but then if the passion is in your heart, you won't want to. It becomes the reason for your existence, and there is no better feeling.

Throughout this book, I've encouraged thinking big. It's all very well to make grand statements, but you can only walk that walk if it's backed up by loving what you do. It is the only way to work harder than anyone else in your field to convert ambition into reality.

And I will not be beaten.

I am fortunate enough in this game to be representing someone I consider to be inspirational. Nobody outworks Anthony Joshua. From his positivity to his commitment and constant hunger to improve, he stands as an example to me. Quite simply, he has made a pact with himself to be the best in all areas of his life.

It isn't only about being a champion in the ring. He's keen to learn Spanish, for example, so he can speak the language during media interviews in Latin America. Nobody told him to do this. There's no obligation. He's done courses on accountancy to give himself a better understanding of his business. This is a world champion sportsman who can employ people to do that for him, but AJ is a cut above the rest. He feels it's his duty to know what's going on, so he can be involved in making informed decisions, and I admire him so much for that.

Boxing is everything to AJ. It's his passion and his life, but that drive to be the best also carries everything that goes with it. Take his sponsorship obligations. He works so hard to fulfil them. I have never seen him moan about it. He's arrived at a promotional shoot after an intense workout to be told he needs to run around the park with one hundred young people. Lesser boxers will die on the inside at the prospect, but not AJ. Even though he's been training hard, he'll join in that run as if there's nowhere else he'd rather be, and those kids will have the time of their lives. It's not a front. Just pure positivity, because he refuses to be outworked, and everyone loves him for it.

AJ and I make a good team. As a boxer and his promoter, we share the same determination. We both want to be at the top of our game, and agree that the only way to achieve greatness is to put the legwork in. AJ sometimes jokes that he could never do what I do, like negotiating contracts at high level, but I don't know how he puts himself through a training regime with such dedication to his craft.

Anybody who pursues their passion is different in that respect, no matter what business they're in, but only the greatest will share that ruthless determination to be the one who works hardest of all.

ROUND 6 – KEY TAKEAWAYS

- Experience is such a valuable asset, no matter what your business ambition. It can provide you with the confidence, knowledge and skills required to work to the best of your ability, and the wisdom to keep it clear and simple at all times.

- In working towards success, there's a lot to be said for simplicity. Your goal might involve many moving parts. If so, strip down each component to serve its intended function. Don't try to be clever if it risks slowing the momentum that you're building to get the job done.

- That sense of relentlessness you need to be successful isn't just something you can summon at will. Nobody wakes up in the morning facing some task that doesn't excite them and thinks, Right, I am going for it! That has to come from within. It's about being massively passionate about your aims and objectives.

- Always think big. It's all very well to make grand statements, but you can only walk that walk if it's backed up by loving what you do. It really is the only way to work harder than anyone else in your field to convert ambition into reality.

Round 7

SELLING THE WORLD

For me, selling is the number one skill in business. It doesn't matter what business you're in, or what you do, it's the most difficult part of the job. Selling is such a pure art. Whether I'm flogging double-glazed windows, the story behind a fight, or securing a billion-dollar TV rights deal, the fundamentals will always remain the same. Selling in all its forms is *the* most important part of the job.

Zig Ziglar, an American salesman and motivational speaker, says that 'selling is essentially a transfer of feelings', and I couldn't agree more. When you believe in your product, when you are emotionally attached to that product and speak with passion and energy, that transfer becomes so much easier to make.

I have been selling since I was a kid. I may not be able to say that I had it rough growing up but selling advertising boards or double glazing is tough. If there was ever a way of learning about rejection, then that is it. In taking knock-back after knock-back, your skin quickly thickens. I can honestly say those moments of trying to get some guy to part with two quid for a fight programme at York Hall, or persuading someone who's hard-pressed to talk to me about investing in new windows, set me up for closing the deal in later life. Those experiences shaped my approach to selling today and taught me what's required to get any deal done.

When we talk about being relentless, that isn't just about your work ethic. For example, in selling, it's about that sick hunger to get a deal over the line. The pursuit of a deal is an addiction in some ways, and one of the biggest challenges in business. Some may downplay its importance, but let's get real. With no sales there's no revenue and ultimately no future for your enterprise. Whether you're selling your product or selling yourself to your manager, speak with passion and confidence and deliver it with a smile. Then, once the job is done, remember your customer and deliver on your promises.

Selling the Dream

I'm a storyteller. As a boxing promoter, my role is to create a narrative around a fight. It isn't simply a question of putting two guys in the ring and making people buy into it. The fact is there's something gladiatorial about an event like this, with drama at every turn. It isn't only about the fight itself, but the build-up. That's where the story unfolds and crucially allows the fans to get behind the fighters.

We're talking about a whole cast here. From the moment the announcement is made, you've got trainers in the mix, the management team, pundits, friends, family, press opinion and even me. We need to understand the boxers' back story, personality and their demons, and sometimes even use this chance to pick a side. We want to know everything that inspires a boxer when they step through the ropes. All kinds of stories come into play in the run-up to a fight, and it's down to me to provide a stage and a spotlight so those tales create maximum excitement and put on a brilliant event.

When I'm setting up the story behind a fight, I always aim to be truthful. That's where the emotions lie, and my job is to bring that out. Good versus bad is great, as is rivalry, but ultimately it's about capturing the imagination. Why? Because when it comes to generating sales, narrative is key. Any sporting event demands a story to engage the audience, whether it's boxing, football, darts or cricket.

Competitors are people. They're human beings. We look at the sacrifices they've made and can identify with their hopes and fears. Loyal fans will always show up when you put on an event, but if you want maximum numbers across all platforms, then you have to showcase the dramas, twists and turns that precede it.

Good storytelling also fuels hype and links it to the product. This doesn't apply only to sport, but every field and industry. Play it right and the narrative you create will strike a chord and bring success. People need to feel invested in the story and the product before they part with their money. A good salesperson has an edge over competitors and keeps customers interested. You have to stay motivated and keep performing the best you can to stay ahead.

In the end, building the right hype around a product, service or event is about connecting people to the human story behind it. With that emotional engagement, you drive interest, expectation, excitement and – crucially – an opportunity to seal the deal.

When it comes to selling, you can't underestimate the importance of good storytelling. Creating a narrative separates you from the competition and gives you a unique selling point in a market that might already be crowded. It's a way to separate you from others and give you a clear identity. People are more receptive to stories than facts or data, so you can't underestimate the importance of this.

As I've already said, I always set out to create a compelling narrative for any fight. My aim is to extract every last drop of value from the story, which is a vital component in making the show a success. Then there are views and opinions to be aired, shared, picked apart or built on. It all adds to the buzz that I aim to build, and to be honest every viewpoint adds value. Good or bad, it serves the same purpose.

I'm a salesman, but I do have to be careful not to blag. If I'm going to stage an event that's as good as I promise, then there has to be substance to that story. It's essential. If it isn't the real deal, if I hype up a show that's never going to deliver, the fans will see through me and then my reputation is on the line. Your reputation is important, and you need to manage that throughout your career. It's crucial if you want to be successful. I can't afford to put myself in that position, but then nor do I need to go there. Why not? Because I believe in every show I put on.

This goes back to what I mentioned earlier about confidence and preparation. When you're confident in your abilities, you're always going to put in the time and preparation to make something a success. That's what I do with every show, and what you need to do too. Whatever it is, whether it's an interview, a meeting, or a task, you need to be fully prepared for every eventuality. Preparation fuels confidence, so the only way you can be sure in your actions is to prepare as much as you can.

Building the Hype, Delivering on Reputation

If I am convinced the fight is going to be massive, a once in a lifetime event, it makes it so much easier for me to sell the narrative behind it. If I'm excited, I sound excited, and that fuels the hype.

What we're talking about here is expectation and excitement. It's a potent mix, but you can't take it for granted. It's easy to talk up a product but if it fails to deliver on its promise, then you lose in every way possible. But when it delivers, your stock can only grow. While we chase the deal, and the buzz that ensues, don't be short-sighted enough to think that's the end goal. Your reputation depends on delivering value for money and what comes with that is the potential of a fruitful relationship with the customer. This is why I always strive to give interviews to anyone who asks. I don't mind if you're the BBC or a YouTuber starting out with a boxing channel and a love of the sport. I will talk to you in order to keep the pages of that story turning, whether it's in the run-up to a fight or the aftermath.

Building the hype is also a way to guarantee immediate sales. If you look at some of the biggest companies in the world, they'll hype up a product months before it's officially released. At Matchroom, we'll do the same but with a fight. We want to make sure that fans are desperate for a fight to happen, that they are counting down the days for when tickets are available. When the link goes live for a fight, I will monitor it multiple times a day. We might have a number of different shows selling at any one time, and if any are lagging, I'm on it. What matters, of course, is that there's true substance behind all the noise.

In creating a show, I think about every element and ask myself what's required to make it truly special. I want the product to deliver on the hype, and I'll look at every aspect of the event to make sure the customer is invested. Understanding the market is key in any trade and you need to make sure that you know it inside out. It makes it so much easier to tailor a product that you know will sell. Nothing is worse than a sales-person trying to sell you something that they don't know much about. You can see straight through it. In boxing, I'm a fan as much as a promoter, and I know that I want this experience to feel special.

Back in the day, watching the boxing with my dad, when a round came to an end there would be silence. When I started staging my own fights, I introduced music. The first time I put on a show and the speakers started blaring, my dad turned to me and yelled, 'What the fuck is this? Turn it down!' I just laughed and asked him to look around. Everyone was out of their seats and dancing.

When hype delivers, your business can only grow. My vision has always been to create shows that people are desperate to be part of. I dress up for the occasion, and others follow suit. We build ringside VIP areas, where celebrities want to be seen. All of a sudden, it's a hot ticket, and if you're lucky enough to get one, your friends are jealous.

What's more, when the fight is as stunning as I believed it would be, those guys who missed out will be in the queue for the next event. Hype and product have come together, and here's my chance to build on it. *The demand has been unbeliev-able*, I'll put out on Twitter next time tickets go on sale. *The pre-sales are through the roof!*

When the buzz is that good, people have been known to have six devices lined up just in case. Then, when they click 'buy' and receive the confirmation, they'll retweet it in a state of excitement or message me to say, 'I've got one!' Then, the customers are building the hype. It's a perfect circle of promotion, but in every case the product has got to be quality.

It's important to note that there is a big difference between hyping a product and overselling it. The former is a compelling tool if you genuinely believe that what you have to offer is sensational. If you know it, and everyone else can buy into it, then there's no limit to where you can take things. A case in point is the ten-figure broadcasting agreement I struck with the streaming giant, DAZN. The deal was breathtaking in size and scope, and effectively gave me the platform and the tools to rebuild boxing in the USA as an entertainment powerhouse.

Naturally, it attracted attention from all over the world. In every interview I gave, however, I maintained with hand on heart that it guaranteed value for money. At this level, there was no room for false promises, and my belief in the future of boxing underpinned every stage of our discussions. It was all about the product, the potential size of the market, and my passion for the vision. Honesty was a key driver here. It removed all scope for doubt and uncertainty, and gave all parties the confidence to move forward together with commitment and conviction.

By contrast, if you're reaching for a reason for someone to buy, then you need to rethink what you're offering. Hype is only effective with substance behind it. Otherwise it's only hot air. Even if your product does meet or exceed expectation, making it a success still demands hard work. Whatever you believe in, the thing you're aiming to sell, you have to be absolutely committed in your mission to take it to the top. You have to be smart. You have to put in more hours than anyone else. You have to be relentless.

Riding the Narrative

Ahead of a show, as momentum builds and the hype starts to build, I have to remain on top of the story. Selling never stops in business, whether it's arena tickets, pay-per-view, or the sense of anticipation that the fans deserve who have already bought into the event. Sometimes, there are so many narrative elements that it's a challenge to keep them all in play.

It doesn't matter what market you are in, a compelling sales narrative is absolutely key in driving numbers. The process has changed. We all now have the ability to communicate much easier with our customers – so why not take advantage? The days of reciting a sales script like a robot are over, the same tired pitch won't ignite the mindset of the next generation, but a good story always will.

When it comes to making a success of anything, in business and in life, you need that storybook to sell the dream. They provide a meaning. You're the author, and it's vital that you make every word count. If you're lost or muddled, everyone loses interest and it's all over. When you're in control, though, it's the best feeling, because it means you're on course to achieve.

In selling a dream, perhaps the greatest challenge of all lies in the fact that the best stories are constantly unfolding. It's essential to be aware of this. If you create a narrative to drive a venture, and then sit back to watch it play out, there's a very good chance it will bite you. Why? Because life is unpredictable. Sometimes, you can work your heart out threading a story that serves to secure a sale or get a deal over the line, only for something unexpected to occur that changes everything completely.

Early in 2019, we announced that Anthony Joshua would be making his American fight debut, defending his unified heavyweight titles against Jarrell 'Big Baby' Miller. In the two years leading up to this, AJ had defended his World Title belts against Carlos Takam, unified his WBA, IBF and WBO World Heavyweight Titles against Joseph Parker, and retained them by stopping Alexander Povetkin in the seventh round at Wembley again. In his own view, AJ was on a knockout streak and looking forward to the challenge from Miller.

The fight was to be staged at Madison Square Garden in New York City. It's an iconic venue, In 1971, Muhammad Ali fought Joe Frazier there in what was billed 'The Fight of the Century'. It's a Mecca for boxing, bang in the middle of Manhattan, and the perfect stage to introduce AJ to the USA.

From the moment I confirmed the fight, the story took off. The guys at Madison Square Garden told me that their phones were ringing before the tickets went on sale. When the lines opened, that fight secured one of the biggest gates created there. At the press conference, Miller shoved AJ before walking off, which was gold dust for the media. Everything was shaping up for the fight to be massive. The buzz kept on building.

Then, with just three weeks left before fight night, I was at home with my wife Chloe and the family when my phone rang. I looked at the name of the caller, and my face fell.

'What's up?' Chloe asked.

I pressed the phone to my ear, focusing hard to filter out the noise of my kids playing. The voice on the other end was familiar to me. She's a lovely lady, but when her name pops up on my screen, I know it's going to be bad news. For all major championship fights, all contenders are subject to random drugs testing by the Voluntary Anti-Doping Association (VADA). A call like this, from the association's headquarters, meant someone had failed a test. In this case, Jarrell Miller's sample had come back positive for a banned steroid. Not once, but three times.

That was it. There are no excuses for this kind of thing.

Miller was done. He was out.

With less than one month to go before one of the biggest fights I had ever staged, with hype and expectation through the roof, Anthony Joshua was the only boxer on the billing. The story had just taken a surprise turn.

I was in shock. I had to process what I'd heard and what that meant going forward. So, I took myself to another room, literally retreating from the fact that I appeared to be completely fucked, and closed the door.

It was one of those moments where I genuinely came close to tears. At the same time, I reminded myself that when life gets tough, you don't run away. You face that ball no matter how hard it's coming at you and aim to knock it for six. In the same way, if I'm selling windows and the guy on the other end of the line tells me to do one, I don't put the phone down. I sympathise that he's having a bad day, and find a way to save it.

If anything, I came to realise, now was the moment that I really had to go to work. If this was meant to challenge me, I would find a way. I had to react and not retreat, I told myself, feeling better as I dug deep for the resolve I would need to face this. The easiest thing in the world would be to pull the fight, heaping all the blame on a boxer who had broken the rules, and then hoping the spotlight stayed on him, but that wasn't my style. This was my responsibility. I had to own it.

In that moment, I wasn't sure how I would save the show. I knew I couldn't back away from this moment. Failure was completely unacceptable to me, I reminded myself, and got back on my feet. I owed it to myself, to Anthony who had worked so hard in training, to the Matchroom family, and all the fans who had joined the journey so far. It meant that even though I was reeling, I knew exactly what the first step needed to be.

I had to get ahead of the story.

People talk in boxing. If one person in the game found out about the failed drugs test, especially someone who didn't like me, then it would leak. I couldn't afford for the news to go public until I had found a replacement for Miller. Why not? Because every fighter worthy of facing AJ in the ring would realise I was desperate, and their price would skyrocket. As soon as they knew I was on the back foot, they could ask for treble, knowing I had no choice.

Pacing the room, I went online and looked at the heavy-weight rankings. It had to be a fighter worthy of facing AJ. There was no way that I would stand some mug for the sake of staging the show, and yet the obvious contenders were contracted elsewhere.

Then I remembered something. A message I had received from Instagram some weeks before. At the time, I had filed it in my mind as something that might have potential one day. Now, with the kids still playing in the other room and the fate of a world champion on my shoulders, it suddenly seemed like a way forward.

Andy Ruiz Jr is an American boxer of Mexican heritage. He had a reputation for taking on big guys and defeating them. He might not look like a giant killer, but I knew he could unleash body shots and upper cuts that have taken down fighters such as Alexander Dimitrenko and Kevin Johnson. Ruiz Jr was also hungry for success, so when a message from him popped up on Instagram, he had my attention. It was brief and to the point, and simply asked me to consider him if any opportunities for a fight came up.

I'm ready, his message to me finished, when I read it again. *Just give me the call.*

I didn't know about his fitness or availability, but I could see that Andy Ruiz Jr might be the solution I so desperately needed. He was a very different challenger to Jarrell Miller, and though his appearance didn't necessarily suggest he could take on AJ, I knew this was a boxer who should not be underestimated. I had to get in touch and hammer out a deal before the news broke about Miller.

So, I went back to him and asked if he'd be interested in fighting the unified heavyweight champ. Of course, this got Andy's attention straight away, and naturally he took it to his agent, his manager and promoter. I was ready for the price to creep up, which it did.

Then I had to take it to AJ and his team, break the news about Miller, and sell this new proposal to them. As one of Anthony's greatest strengths is his intelligence, he understood the situation. He was also well aware of Ruiz Jr's form and potential, and recognised that we needed to get this deal done as a matter of urgency.

When Anthony agreed, I took an offer to Ruiz's people and sealed the deal. We signed contracts and made the official announcement. Following Miller's dismissal from the billing, Anthony Joshua would still be defending his title on 1 June at Madison Square Garden. I had snatched victory from the jaws of defeat, and it felt sweet.

I couldn't afford for one moment to sit back as if I had done my job. If anything, the story had only just begun.

To the hardcore boxing fan, Andy Ruiz Jr was a fighter worthy of facing the very best boxers in the ring. When it came to the casual viewer, however, I had an image problem to overcome. In one corner we had Anthony Joshua, who looked like an Adonis, and in the other there was Ruiz Jr . . . who didn't.

With his belly wobbling over his shorts, Andy hardly seemed like a fighter worthy of being in the opposite corner. Sure enough, when he was announced as Miller's replacement, there were a few moans and some refunds to pay out. I had some hard selling to do in introducing Ruiz Jr to the public, but the momentum was still there for AJ to defend his belts.

The story had taken an unexpected twist, but if anything that fired up even more interest. Had I let it slip from my fingers, and watched the news break about Miller before I'd found a replacement, I would have failed. Instead, with the unexpected drama resolved before it went public, I had a new edge to the narrative.

It was exciting. I was buzzing about the fight, and that played out in the interviews I gave in the run up to the event. Ruiz Jr was no fall guy. This was a genuine contender and so when it came to selling that show, I did so with the only thing that will guarantee success: *passion*.

No Passion, No Point

We all recognise the importance of drive and motivation in the pursuit of success. You've got to have the right mindset to take on all challenges and stay focused on the targets that you've set yourself, but critically you have to believe in what you're selling.

Without it, if you sound hollow or half-hearted, and the transfer of emotions is lost. I put 110 per cent into all the shows I stage, because I know they're going to be incredible. It doesn't matter what boxer you're backing, this is a fight worth watching and the experience is going to be intense. The venue is iconic, it'll be packed out, and you'll remember this for a long time to come. That's what motivates me to stand up and sell the show, because it's coming from the heart.

Not every product has the potential to light up the world, of course. Here's an example: I could be travelling up and down the country every week selling printers. For one thing, that's hardly a piece of kit that sets the pulse racing. What's more, the brand I'm representing might be a bit crap. The ink cartridges dry up quickly and the paper jams. Whatever. Yes, I could blag it, but unless I truly believe in that printer in some shape or form, then true success will never come my way. If there's no passion, then seriously what's the point?

Being passionate is one of the most important things you need to be successful. It fuels excitement and drives confidence. Passion drives you to succeed because you are completely dedicated to making it work, no matter how hard things might be. Steve Jobs said, 'the only way you do great work is to love what you do' and I couldn't agree more. When you believe in what you're doing, you don't have to pretend to be anything other than yourself. If you're committed to the product, the project or the company, that's when your true nature shines and works in your favour. As soon as you begin to love what you do, and achieve happiness at work, positivity and happiness start spreading to other areas of your life.

I used to represent a fighter called Tommy Coyle. He's a lovely guy with a solid family. His dad, Chris, owns a fruit stall in Hull. What sets him apart from all the other fruit sellers is that Chris believes his product is the very best in the north-east of the country. If you visit his stall – and I've done so and even had a crack at selling – his enthusiasm is infectious. Chris believes he can't be beaten for freshness or value for money, and before you know it, you've got a punnet in your possession and a smile on your face.

Now, staging a fight at Wembley Stadium in front of 90,000 people might be on a different scale to selling strawberries in the market, but the fundamentals are the same. They always are with selling. It's all about believing in the product, because the passion that drives it is what brings you the results.

I believed in Andy Ruiz Jr. I genuinely saw him as a worthy opponent to Anthony Joshua. From the moment we made the announcement, I was behind that fight every step of the way. If you watch boxing promoters at a press conference, almost always they'll stand in front of the media with notes in their hand. Some of the worst offenders will simply read from a script they've prepared earlier. They might stumble over names or get muddled over dates and it sounds dreadful. Monotone and dull.

Not once in my career have I spoken at a press conference with notes. For me, it's become my trademark. There might be ten fights on the card. I'll know the name and history of every fighter. I'll know their highlights, low moments, fears and expect-ations. In short, I believe what I'm selling, but it's not through sitting at home memorising it all beforehand. I know it because I'm passionate about the sport. I love it. I've picked it up through watching these fighters progress through their own stories. Talk to any fan and they'll reel off facts and figures with the same enthusiasm, which is what I bring with me to the press confer-ences. I believe in the product I have to offer and want to share that passion with you. It's important to remember that by being passionate and enthusiastic, others will begin to get excited. It can only help your cause.

When it came to pitching Ruiz Jr as a replacement for Miller, then, I had to find the hook. Somehow, I needed to get the public to see beyond his waistline and recognise that this fighter had the potential to be massive. With a human story in mind, I began with the account of how Andy came onto my radar. I told the tale of how a message on Instagram led to a world-class heavyweight fight that nobody could afford to miss. I even embraced the fact that he wasn't in the best shape to flag up the fact that he shouldn't be underestimated. It wasn't something to hide. It was further fuel for the narrative. If it burned, I used it.

'Can I ask you how it would feel,' I asked Ruiz Jr at the press conference we convened to announce him as the new contender, 'if you were crowned Mexico's very first heavyweight world champion?'

I'll be honest, I don't think he'd even thought about it. This guy had gone from a punt on social media to a shot at the World Title, but to be fair he ran with it.

'This has always been my dream,' he replied, and that went around the world.

A little part of me wished I hadn't said that, because Andy turned that into the legacy he was chasing. Then again, he was a likeable guy and it helped the story gather momentum. In particular, it tapped into Hispanic support, which is both passionate and huge. Even though Ruiz is American, he is proud of his Mexican heritage. All of a sudden, Andy was the focus of wild celebrations among Mexicans and in turn that drove subscribers to DAZN, who were broadcasting the fight. He had a mariachi band at the weigh-in, which gave him so much character and ultimately reinforced the narrative.

Could this Mexican guy defeat the reigning world champ?

Looking back, I'm not sure that many people really thought he could, but everyone loved the story. Even though what followed took everyone by surprise, I had sold a dream that I was genuinely passionate about, and delivered it to the world.

ROUND 7 – KEY TAKEAWAYS

- Selling is the number one skill in business. Unless you understand that and its art, then I don't believe you can run a successful business. Over the years, whether I've been flogging double glazing, making people buy into the story of a big fight, or securing a billion-dollar TV rights deal, the fundamentals will always remain the same.

- Some may downplay the importance of sales, particularly those who don't excel at the skill, but let's get real – no sales, no business. Whether you are selling the product or selling yourself, you have to speak with passion and confidence, and always deliver it with a smile. Once the job is done, remember your customer and deliver on your promises.

- While the mindset must be right to take on these challenges, critically you must believe in what you are selling. If not, you may sound hollow and half-hearted, and the transfer of emotions to your customer is lost.

- Expectation and excitement is a potent mix, but you can't take it for granted. It's easy to talk up a product, but if it fails to deliver on its promise, you lose in every way possible. When it delivers, though, your stock can only grow. While you chase the deal and the buzz that ensues, don't be short-sighted enough to think that is the end goal. Your reputation depends on delivering value for money, and with that comes the potential of a fruitful relationship with the customer.

Round 8

THE TEAM IN YOUR CORNER

Our Family, Our Business, Our Rules

Recently, my dad created a mission statement for Matchroom. This is how it reads:

> *Our job is to create opportunities for sportsmen and women with as few barriers to entry as possible, to have fun and make a profit. We judge ourselves on prize money levels, tournament numbers, TV ratings and profit.*
>
> *We value our staff, and if they deliver either in extra effort or extra profitability, we reward them properly.*
>
> *We have a plan for each event, a short and long term strategy, and we do not waver from that plan unless we experience changing circumstances.*
>
> *We do not listen to uninformed criticism.*
>
> *We always over deliver, and our handshake is better than any contract.*
>
> *We are honest and legal, with integrity in all we do.*
>
> *We are on a mission from God. We are relentless.*
>
> *We accept we will make dozens of mistakes, but we will make thousands of decisions.*

We never say we are the best sports promoter in the world, but we know we are in a group of one.

We love our jobs. It is not a quick fix. It is a long-term marriage.

We pay our way, no charity, no handouts, just graft.

We tell the truth. We can afford to and that's a luxury.

We think poor in everything we do. We want value for money and so do our clients.

We go the extra mile and no one can ever live with our work ethic.

We understand everything ends one day, and so we'll enjoy every second of it.

There is never any complacency in our lives.

We acknowledge how lucky we are.

We are a special family.

Matchroom aren't the only company to create something like this. Putting values into words can be useful in providing focus for the team. It serves as a reminder of what lies at the core of a business, helping individuals and departments to align around it.

What's significant about the mission statement my dad wrote is that he didn't create it primarily for the office. He had two copies printed and framed, which he gave to my young daughters as Christmas presents.

From an outside point of view, this might seem like an unusual gift. Through my eyes, it sums up our relationship with both business and family. Both are central to our lives and we're fully invested in them. In many ways, they're indivisible – when it comes to Matchroom, work is family. Ultimately, the values we hold dear apply to my daughters as much as my team. It's all about bonds and a shared belief.

Of course, not everyone reading this book will be a business owner. Without a doubt, it is difficult for an employee to share the same passion and drive as the employer who started from scratch. As we'll see, however, it's still possible to be part of a team where a sense of purpose and belonging unites, inspires, and strengthens the drive for success.

One Family

If you build a business from the hull up, and employ people to help crew your journey to success, then effectively you are captain of a ship. There can be only one person at the wheel, which means the fate of the vessel and everyone on board rests with you.

As the captain, you're in command and riding the waves. When that ship hits a storm, it falls to you to chart a safe passage. Naturally, you want a team you can depend upon, standing strong with you. The last thing you need as the waves crash over the deck is for dissenting voices to ask what the fuck they're doing out there.

It can happen under pressure. If someone is in a role they don't love, and conditions are testing, it's only natural for them to wish they were elsewhere. So, if you want to make it to the promised land, no matter how far away it may be or what lies ahead, it's your responsibility to create an environment on board that guarantees loyalty and commitment. Everyone needs to feel invested in the destiny of this ship. They want to feel valued for their contribution and, as a result, they will be prepared to do whatever it takes to help achieve your goals.

At Matchroom, we don't demand the values required from staff to make our business a success. We create an environment where they take those values to heart. People work to the best of their abilities when they're motivated. Part of that comes down to money, of course, but feeling valued is equally important. That's what encourages employees to give 110 per cent. Recognition for great work is a motivating force. It encourages drive, positivity and ambition, and if everyone shares the same commitment to achieving a vision, it brings people closer together. Bonded by loyalty, that's when we can start to consider the business as family.

My dad started Matchroom on his own. He always wanted me to join him, but understood that I had to feel that I'd earned the position. My sister is also in the business, and there's no doubt that we bring our family values to work. We're a tight unit at home. Family meals are important, for example, especially on a Sunday. Even now, if you're not there, it doesn't go down well. Every time Dad and I start talking business, Mum shouts and screams, there's a short pause and then we glance at each other.

'Anyway, that deal you done . . .'

Whether we're gathered around the dining table or in the boardroom, we bring that passion with us. It might annoy my mum for a moment, but she knows that that our energy and commitment to Matchroom also benefits the family. It isn't all about money, as is evident in the framed prints in my daughters' bedrooms. It's about upholding values. That is the binding element. When shared, they bring people together – whether you're at home or in the workplace.

Opportunity Is Everything

We're a family business that has grown to become an international brand, and yet we still recruit at a junior level. Our aim is to give those individuals the space and support to prove themselves as they work their way up through the business. As a result, our senior team have effectively been with us since they set out on their careers. I'm proud of the fact that they have chosen to grow with us, because time and experience grows trust. It gives me the confidence to know that they're fully invested in driving forward the company.

Frank Smith has been working for me since he was fifteen. When I first met him, he was a schoolkid trying to flog me raffle tickets at a party. I gave him twenty quid for the tickets and never expected to see him again. Five minutes later, he was back. Someone had told him that I owned the Bentley outside and now he wanted to press more money out of me. I had to admire him for it, so when he applied for work experience at Matchroom, I gave him the opportunity.

Frank started out making the tea and doing the photocopying – that sort of thing. When he left school, I knew he could work hard, and was hungry to make something of his life. So, I gave a him a full-time shot. I had to warn him once for oversleeping, but he learned and matured and took on more responsibilities over a dozen-odd years, until now he's my Chief Executive.

When Frank joined Matchroom, I'd only just started out as a boxing promoter. As my right-hand man in the division, Frank had to take on new challenges and master them, like I did. He cut his teeth on fighter contracts, selling rights to our broadcast partners, and manages the global boxing teams day-to-day across all aspects. He's spent his entire professional life with Matchroom. He lives and breathes the same values as me and I trust him with everything.

As an employer, there is nothing more rewarding than to see an employee make personal sacrifices for the business. Frank lives an amazing life thanks to Matchroom. He flies all over the world, with ringside seats at top-level fights, but he missed out on university and nights out with the lads. It's his choice, of course, but he has made that sacrifice and commitment to me, and I have recognised it and rewarded him. It isn't only about salary, but awarding more responsibilities, knowing that he'll deliver.

Frank has shown me that he has what it takes to be central to this business, and that opportunity is available to everyone who works at Matchroom.

As a business in the public eye, I receive a lot of CVs from young hopefuls. *I'm a go-getter*, it might begin, which gets my attention, or *You won't find anyone more hard-working than me.* I rarely spend much time looking at an applicant's history. I'm more interested in the spirit of the correspondence. In the same way, if I invite someone in for an interview, then I tend to focus on their energy. It's a quality in people that tells you they can make things happen. In an environment with opportunity, especially working in a field they love, that energy can drive passion, focus and commitment. For me, it's a measure of someone's potential to be a valuable member of the team.

The energy you project and put out into the workplace is important. It can determine the outcome of an interview, a meeting, or even your company. Why? Because it shows that you want to make something of the opportunity presented to you. You want to get on, and that's evident in the way you present yourself.

Of course, anyone can say the right thing to earn the opportunity. But then it's a question of proving themselves, and I will be watching. If my guy starts his window cleaning round, finishes a client's house and then drops flyers through neighbouring letter boxes, I'll be impressed. Should they keep it up,

I might even give them the tools to create a promotional campaign. On the other hand, if my apprentice jumps in the van after the first customer, only to park it up the road because they've got time for a fag and a nap, then they're unlikely to see out their probation period.

With commitment comes reward. It's as simple as that.

If you want to be successful and achieve your goals, hard work is the most important thing. I can't stress that enough. You won't get anywhere without working hard. When you start to pursue your goals with relentless drive, then you begin to separate yourself from the competition. There might be times in your life when you're not the most talented, but there can be no excuses for not being the hardest worker. There's a saying that goes 'hard work beats talent when talent doesn't work'. It's down to you to make something happen.

Trust in Leadership

You might have what it takes to be successful on your own terms. Your mindset's in the right place, your positivity, passion, focus and drive. You're so hungry for the win that it's a constant craving, and that's great, but what if you can't reach your goal alone?

In this situation, it doesn't matter how driven you might be, you have to be able to assemble a band of people you trust to deliver on your vision.

In building a team, I give responsibility to people with the potential to shine. In doing so, however, that often means handing over something I would normally do myself. I'll admit, I find this hard sometimes. Everything I have built in boxing has my stamp on it. With the business growing along with my vision for the future, I have to delegate. There's a temptation to micro-manage, but ultimately that does me, my employees and the business no favours. Nothing thrives that way. It's suffocating, and that will be reflected in your overall success.

It's only lately that I've embraced delegation, and made it something that works for everyone. Matchroom's fight posters are a case in point, which might seem like such a small thing but, until recently, I used to design them myself. It goes back to my arrival on the scene as a boxing promoter. I looked around at the worn-out bill posters my rivals were plastering up in underpasses and knew that I could do better. I had a quality show to sell, which meant creating an image that demanded attention. It became my stamp, with a compelling title for the show, prime boxers, lightning, blood . . . whatever made you stop in your tracks and think, *Fuck me, I'm having that!*

Today, we're staging forty shows a year. I don't have the time to focus my attention on creating the very best poster at this scale, and so we employ designers. These guys are at the top of their game. They're dedicated to their craft, but for a while I couldn't leave it alone. I'd be asking for last-minute changes that risked a poster not being ready for a press conference, which stressed everyone out. Eventually, I realised that I had to change. My priority was in driving the business forwards. If I wanted to continue at full tilt, I needed to have faith in my team.

It's never too late to learn. There's no other way to improve in life. For me, as the guy in charge, it was the realisation that I didn't need to impose my personal stamp on everything. Instead, I switched my attention to nurturing those people around me – many of whom are specialists in their field – to understand what I needed and to give them the freedom to thrive. It's about giving your team the space, time and tools, along with the insight they require to understand the course you've charted. Not only do you get what you want on time, it establishes trust, a sense of reward and responsibility, and encourages your team to pull as one.

By building and establishing trust within your team, you will reap the rewards. When a team knows they can trust each other, it creates an environment in which morale increases, productivity rises, and everything becomes overwhelmingly positive. Nobody wants to work with people who they don't trust because that kind of negativity will affect your business. Be sure to establish a culture in which each team member is viewed as a valuable asset, and has a clear identity.

On Loyalty

Emily Frazer has been with Matchroom for a decade now. She's an incredible asset to the company, brimming with enthusiasm and efficiency. Having started making the teas and coffees, she's worked her way up to becoming the managing director of Matchroom's Multi Sport. She's exactly the right person to drive this division, and I can't wait to see what she does with it. The reason I mention this here is because recently Emily marked her time with us with a tweet, in which she said, quite simply, 'Matchroom is in my blood.'

I read this and felt the hairs on the back of my neck stand on end.

For a team member to say that our family business means that much is such an honour. It validates everything we do for our staff. I also think it speaks volumes about loyalty. Blood is a strong symbol when it comes to pledging allegiance, but it has to be earned. No business owner can expect that from their employees simply by giving them a job. That's only the start of the journey.

As a business leader, my dad is very good at making people understand what Matchroom is about. That's an essential attribute in building a team in step with your aims and ambitions. Not only that, Dad is exceptional in the way he treats our employees.

'We must look after them,' he's always saying to me, because he knows what role that plays in getting the very best from people. Salary plays a part here, and if we've performed well as a business, that's reflected in the bonuses. A good business owner should value their staff – not just monetarily – and never take them for granted. It's the cost of motivation, and a price worth paying to maintain momentum and growth.

Like my old man, I also believe that creating a sense of 'togetherness' can bond a team. At Matchroom, it's us against the world, and if we're going to put on a great show that means we pull together. It's not only about me, but everyone in the team. Nobody is overlooked for their efforts – hard work is always recognised. A team with a strong identity can thrive.

Fight weekend is the end stage of a long journey for everyone in the team. It's also an intensely busy phase as the team ensures that everything is in place. This isn't a nine-to-five experience. They're working Friday, Saturday, Sunday, and going above and beyond what has to be done. In return, I will look after my people. We'll stay at a nice hotel and go out for a meal on the eve of the fight and celebrate a great show. At the final press conference, I'll thank everyone by name for the amazing work they've done.

There's still lots to address on the Sunday, of course, but the pressure is off and we can have a laugh as we pack up and head home. It's a great experience all round, and come Monday, everyone will be at their desks first thing. Why? Because our focus shifts to the next event and the obstacles we must overcome to make it even bigger and better.

What we don't do at Matchroom, however, is time off in lieu. Working through a weekend isn't some kind of exception to the nine-to-five for us. It's part of the job, which is devoted to putting on the best show possible and doing whatever it takes to deliver that. If someone comes up to me and asks for the Monday off, having enjoyed a great weekend with financial, professional and personal rewards, then they're in the wrong job. My team have fun, but make no mistake, they work hard.

The best companies employ people who genuinely want to be there. I can think of nothing worse than going to work and hating it. Yes, there are some who consider a job to be a means to an end, often to pursue some personal goal in their free time, and that's fine. But the last thing I want is individuals working for me who are miserable or unmotivated. I have to ensure that I get the best from people, which is why we create a working environment that feels like a place you'd want to be.

Matchroom now occupies the house where I grew up. Even though my sister, our parents and I moved on years ago, it's still a family home – except there are forty of us under the roof now. It's big and spacious, with a swimming pool and a gym, which we encourage staff to use. It's not a spa, but if you want people to go the extra mile, first they have to feel happy in the workplace.

Then, if someone from accounts emails me with a suggestion as to how we can optimise our spend across hotels – something beyond their job role – I can't tell you how much that will impress me. It shows individual initiative and a commitment to the company, and chances are I will invite that person to put the plan into practice. It's their project, and an opportunity to rise to the challenge and make a difference to the business. I really encourage you, in whatever you do, to volunteer ideas to your employer off your own back. Be brave and back yourself. If you've got a good idea or you spot an opportunity within your business, then make a point of flagging it. It's such an easy win, but I promise it will put you on their radar.

Motivation, responsibility and reward. With these three pillars in place, you can create a loyal team that will do whatever it takes to drive your vision. And if that team feels like family, you can't ask for more than that.

ROUND 8 – KEY TAKEAWAYS

- When you start to dedicate yourself fully to achieving your goals, you begin separating yourself from the competition. It's about the work you put in. There might be times when you're not the most talented person in the room, but there can be no excuses for not being the hardest worker.

- There comes a time when you might not be able to reach your goals on your own. When this happens, it's about developing and nurturing a strong team. Giving responsibility to those around you establishes trust, a sense of responsibility, and encourages you all to pull as one towards the end goal.

- Trust in a team is so important. Nobody wants to work with people they don't trust because that negativity will affect you and your business. You have to establish a culture in which each member is viewed as a valuable asset. Only then can you all flourish.

Round 9

SETBACKS PAVE THE WAY FOR COMEBACKS

In boxing, if a fighter drops their guard or concentration for a split second, then they risk taking a heavy blow which will quite often lead to defeat. Outside the ring, business operates on much the same basis. In pursuing any goal, focus and preparation is key. It's great to be big, bold and ambitious, but without constant focus you risk getting hurt.

When it comes to recovering your composure or even climbing back on your feet, there's a lot to be learned from the sport of boxing. Some of the greatest fighters have suffered crushing defeats and then come back stronger.

In business, regaining your composure after a damaging blow demands a huge amount of self-belief. It also requires brains as well as brawn, because unless you've learned a lesson from the experience, you risk making the same mistake again.

In the pursuit of success, it's only realistic that we address those moments when everything doesn't go to plan. It can happen, which is why it's so important to develop the mindset and strategies to learn lessons and grow stronger for the experience.

Lessons Learned

Nobody likes making mistakes in business. If I get something wrong, I feel that I've let myself down, because I should've been sharper.

At the same time, if you're pushing for success and something goes wrong on your watch, that's exactly how you should feel. If it doesn't weigh heavily on you, then perhaps you need to review how emotionally invested you are in the business itself. Complacency is a sure-fire way for mistakes to happen. It's second only to greed. If you're tempted to coast or make a cash grab from a project, then the focus you need to deliver on quality will slip.

There are all sorts of ways we can drop our guard, but for whatever reason we make a mistake, it hurts – because there's no going back. It can't be undone. These moments can be costly, inside the boxing ring and out of it, but when processed with the right attitude, they can also contribute to long-term success.

On a balmy night in Manhattan, on 1 June 2019, in front of a crowd wired for excitement, two heavyweight fighters faced each other in the ring. What followed would prove to be one of the greatest upsets in boxing history. Anthony Joshua had come to Madison Square Garden to defend his titles against the underdog, Andy Ruiz Jr. After the drama caused by Jarrell Miller dropping out after failing three drugs tests, we had kept the show on the road by replacing him with a boxer who divided opinion.

As a proud Mexican American, Ruiz Jr had the Mexican fanbase that made him hugely popular. He also had a history of fights that highlighted what a danger he could pose, and yet there was no ignoring the fact that he had a belly on him. Compared to Joshua with his sculpted body and a height advantage, Ruiz Jr was a different contender. I had every faith in AJ. I knew how hard he'd worked for this moment, but unlike so many people, I never underestimated his opponent.

For a fight story that had taken an unexpected turn, it seemed the narrative still had a sting in the tail. While Ruiz found himself on the canvas in round three, he came back hard and exploited the slightest drop in AJ's guard. It was a rare moment for Anthony, who took his turn on the deck, and never fully recovered. In the seventh round he paid the price, having suffered a third brutal assault from the Mexican American. AJ picked himself up and retreated to the corner ropes to compose himself, but it was too late. The referee looked him in the eyes, didn't like what he saw, and called it.

In that moment, as Ruiz Jr bounced around in victory, a sense of shock gripped the fans in the arena. I looked up at AJ; he was gracious in defeat, but the fire that burned inside him had dimmed. Minutes later, I was interviewed in the ring about what we had just witnessed. I conceded that Anthony had been sloppy, and yet I had no doubt that the spark inside him would soon burn. There would be a rematch, I promised the fans and the viewers at home, while thinking at the same time that this crushing defeat would have massive consequences for us all.

In sport, you win and lose and that's exactly my attitude in business. Boxers win fights and they lose them. That's the game. As a promoter, I want to see a close fight with no guaranteed outcome, and so do the fans. AJ was no exception to that rule, but his star had shone so brightly since winning Olympic gold that people had begun to see him as unbeatable. His fight against Ruiz Jr was great viewing, but potentially his stock value had also taken a beating. Moving forward, I knew that could hurt the company, and I wasn't going to let it happen.

Sometime around three in the morning, I finally left MSG. My driver was waiting outside. I looked at him and said, 'You know what mate; I'm going to have a walk.'

He asked where I was going to walk to.

'Back to the hotel,' I said.

'Are you sure? It's a long way.' He couldn't believe it.

It was about five miles back to the hotel, but it was a warm evening and I needed the air. New York is always pretty special after dark, but I walked back in a daze. Some of the fans were still out, celebrating or commiserating, and that included quite a few Brits. I shared a few words with those who recognised me. Even then, I promised AJ would be back.

Back home, as AJ regrouped from his defeat, I focused on maintaining momentum at Matchroom. I had a fight in mind that appealed to the hardcore fan in me. I knew it could be absolute dynamite, pitting our own Luke Campbell against Vasyl Lomachenko from Ukraine, holder of three World Lightweight Titles and widely considered the best pound-for-pound fighter on the planet,

Lomachenko wasn't that well known to the casual viewer, but to the fan he was a god. He's one of the most gifted fighters in the world right now. He'd never boxed in the UK before, and I wanted to be the one who brought him over. Then there was Campbell, a 2012 Team GB Olympic gold medallist, who's one of the mostly highly regarded fighters in his division. As a pairing, it was perfect. With critics beginning to mutter that Matchroom were done following AJ's defeat, because the company and the fighter were so closely tied, I wanted to show them we had only just begun.

How? By bringing fucking Lomachenko to the O2 Arena in London for the fight of his life!

We earned a lot of plaudits for delivering that fight, which took place two months after that night in New York. Campbell took Lomachenko the full twelve rounds. It ended in defeat, but the boxing was sensational, and full credit to him for that. With the weekend done, my team and I returned to the office on Monday. There, I took a look at the numbers.

Securing both fighters had been expensive. At the same time, the pay-per-view numbers were never going to rival the Joshua/Ruiz Jr fight. We sold out the O2 to the hardcore fans, desperate to watch Lomachenko live, but the fact remained these guys weren't household names. As a result, as we crunched the figures, they weren't even close to where I needed them to be.

In assembling the show, I had said to myself that if I broke even I'd be over the moon. For the sake of a quality fight that reminded fans that Matchroom were at the forefront of boxing, I'd have taken a loss of two or even three hundred grand. We could've swallowed it, knowing that the fans were still with us moving forwards. But as we processed the takings and the outgoings, it became clear that I had lost over half a million quid.

And that ate me up.

The money was one thing, but the fact that I'd thrown away an opportunity to hit my target was unforgivable to me.

'Well, you live and learn,' said my dad when I went to see him, even though I'd seen him miss a blink when he looked at the figures. 'You live and learn.'

'I know, but with AJ losing, I felt we had to—'

'It's done,' he cut in. 'Next time, Ed, you just got to be smarter.'

Even with Dad's advice, I struggled with that loss. It was painful. I took responsibility for it, of course – the whole thing was on me. Brooding on what had gone wrong, reflecting on how I'd approached that show, I realised that like AJ, I could have been better. With this awareness, as with any business owner on the ropes, I vowed that I would never allow myself to be in this position again.

Review and Revitalise

The only way to come to terms with a mistake is by learning from the experience. I admit I don't find it easy to let go of these things. Even now, the loss from the Lomachenko fight unsettles me. It's not the money, but the fact that I got it wrong. It's very easy to look back and wish you'd done things differently. What matters, in any situation like this, is that you understand what went wrong so you don't repeat the same mistake in future.

I spent a great deal of time reflecting on how I put that show together. In many ways, in the aftermath of the Madison Square Garden fight, I was reeling in the same way as AJ. My head was clouded by the loss, and as a result I let my ego get ahead of me. I set my sights on bringing Lomachenko to the UK as a means of proving myself.

In retrospect, my motivation wasn't in the right place. My focus was on the prestige more than the business. Then there was the fee for securing the Ukrainian. Could I have done so for a little less? Probably. Did I spend too much on flights and hotels? Yes, I did. Should we have staged the workouts and the press conferences somewhere a little bit cheaper . . . I went through the list and realised my focus was on making this a top flight event without due care for the bottom line, and that had come back to hurt me.

This wasn't a fight that was ever going to produce incredible numbers. Even so, I had not met the standard I expected of myself. I obsessed over it for a while, because I measure my performance in terms of targets, and you should too. Setting goals gives you long-term vision and short-term motivation. It focuses your mindset and helps you organise your time and resources so you can get the most out of life. Setting clearly defined goals, you can measure and take pride in achieving them. You can see the progress you're making in what might have originally seemed a long and pointless grind. I set a goal for myself annually, not as an end point but a marker on a greater journey, and each one has to be bigger than the last. Then, everything I do is designed to propel me to that target and even beyond. With the Lomachenko fight, I fell short. As a company, with so many events and income streams, we wouldn't notice. On a personal level, it was a blow.

It's here that a sense of positivity has to kick in. In overcoming any mistake you have to use that experience – and the pain that goes with it if your business is central to your life – and accept that you're not too old or wise to keep learning. This way, the mistake has value.

I couldn't go back in time to turn the screw a little tighter as I set up that fight, but I had filed it in my memory. Should I ever find myself in a similar situation, staging a fight that's compelling but may be commercially challenging, I'll think, *Hmm, Lomachenko/Campbell.* I'll still focus on putting on a great show, but with a firmer hand on the budgets.

Learning from mistakes is the only way to find acceptance about what's happened. It's important mentally as well, because if you're simply stewing, then you're still on the canvas. You need to get back on your feet, recover your composure, assess what went wrong and then return to battle stronger for the experience.

Whatever business you're in, we're only human. Nobody wants to make a mistake, but your true measure comes from how you handle it. And if there's one man who knows how to overcome a setback and make an explosive return, it's Anthony Joshua.

Coming Back Stronger

You can't plan for setbacks. If you've done all the preparation, and put your heart and soul into a venture, then on paper there shouldn't be anything down the line that can derail you.

In reality, however, and especially in the ring, all it takes is one lapse of concentration and you're done. The fact is you'll never know what impact a mistake will have until you make it, which is why they should never be ignored. Make the same mistake twice in sport or business and you don't deserve success. Use the experience to future-proof your performance, and the lessons learned can be invaluable.

When AJ lost his heavyweight titles at MSG, he handled the defeat with incredibly good grace. When Ruiz and his team stopped dancing around the ring, Anthony hugged and congratulated him and then posed for photos together. There was no skulking or sulking – his good grace shone through. Back in his changing room, while the doctor assessed him physically, I knew that on the inside Josh was hurting very badly.

'You alright?' I asked.

'Yeah,' he said. 'It happens.'

There was little more to be said in that moment. The doctor was concerned that AJ had a concussion.

'I'll handle the press conference,' I told him. 'You just take your time here.'

AJ looked up at me.

'I'm coming,' he said, only for the doctor to insist he rest.

So, I went upstairs to where the media were waiting. I repeated what I'd said in the ring about our desire to exercise the Immediate Rematch clause, which obligated Ruiz to defend his newly acquired titles. I was honest in my assessment of the fight. AJ had left the door ajar for Ruiz to slam it open, and from there he wasn't going to leave. At the same time, I stressed that AJ would reflect deeply on this loss, rebuild and refocus. This wasn't merely spin, because the story was set to continue. It was exactly how the big man would respond to this major setback. He was fighting for his career now, but knowing him as well as I did, my faith in him held strong.

Afterwards, I returned to the dressing room to check on Anthony. Boxers put their lives on the line every time the bell rings for the round, and AJ had taken several big shots to the head. I found him sitting quietly, deep in thought.

'Are there any media left up there?' he asked me.

I assumed that he was hoping to make a quiet exit. When I told him a few were bound to wait until they were kicked out, AJ rose to his feet.

'The doctor told you to rest,' I reminded him.

'We're doing this,' he said, and led the way to the door.

Towards one o'clock in the morning, ages after the crowds had left, AJ spent a whole hour with the remaining press. He was honest in his interviews, making no excuses for his performance while acknowledging Ruiz Jr as a deserving champion. At one point, a journalist departed from his script and spoke his mind.

'AJ, it's late, you lost the fight.' He gestured at the last remaining journalists awaiting time with him, and I knew what he was thinking. Any other defeated boxer would've made their excuses and gone long ago. 'Why are you still here?'

AJ smiled and shrugged.

'I can't expect one thing when I win and another when I lose,' he said. 'I've got to be the same individual. I have to do the same things.'

There's a lot of things you can learn from AJ. One thing is his humility. If you want to be successful, you have to set aside your ego and be able to reflect on the past and what's happened. If you don't, you will miss opportunities presented to you because you won't be open to new ideas or input. You have to be positive and be able to move forward and adjust to changes that come your way. You can make progress, become a better person, and achieve success.

In the momentum we had worked so hard to build towards this fight, I hadn't considered how I might feel if AJ lost. It had been a challenging night, and yet that didn't involve dealing with an inconsolable boxer who had suffered a shock defeat. If anything, AJ had shown us all how to conduct ourselves in the face of a setback.

When things don't go to plan, positivity is your lifeline. You still have to do some soul-searching, and recognise what went wrong, but in that moment of despair, it's vital that you remind yourself of your long-term aims and ambitions. And if that demands that you raise your game, then that's exactly what you do.

The next morning, I decided to visit AJ at the apartment where he was staying. Part of me wondered whether his good grace the night before had been a front. I half-expected to find him looking broken, and I was ready for things to be grim.

Instead, AJ welcomed me in as if he'd retained his titles in that ring. Deep down, I knew he was torn up by what had happened, and yet he had not let go of the determination and commitment to be the best that had guided him throughout his career.

'We go again,' he said to me quite simply, when I asked what was next. 'But first I have to be better.'

We took our conversation outside onto the balcony. It was another hot day in New York with clear blue skies overhead. There, AJ asked me what I thought about the situation.

'You lost,' I said frankly. 'You weren't expecting to, but he's contracted to a rematch. You can win those belts back, and I promise you I will make sure you get that opportunity.'

'But I have to work harder,' said AJ.

I told him not to be too tough on himself.

'Nobody works as hard as you,' I said.

AJ heard me, but there was one thing on his mind that morning, which he repeated over and over.

I have to be better.

It was a mantra that would guide AJ through the months that followed, and which I applied to myself in the aftermath of the Lomachenko/Campbell fight. In the relentless pursuit of success, there is no other way forward. It's about constantly striving to improve, without excuses for what has gone before, and every confidence that the experience and your ability will take you to another level in the future.

ROUND 9 – KEY TAKEAWAYS

- When it comes to recovering your composure or even climbing back on your feet, there's a lot to be learned from the sport of boxing. Some of the greatest fighters have suffered devastating, humiliating defeats, and then come back stronger. In business, regaining your composure after a damaging blow demands a huge amount of self-belief. It also requires brains as well as heart, because unless you've learned a lesson from the experience, you risk making the same mistake and walking onto that big left hook all over again.

- In the pursuit of success, it's only realistic that we address those moments when everything doesn't go to plan. It can happen, which is why it's so important to develop the mindset and strategies to learn lessons and grow stronger from the experience.

- When things don't go to plan, positivity is your lifeline. You must still do some soul-searching, and recognise what went wrong, but in that moment of despair it's vital that you remind yourself of your long-term aims and ambitions. It's during those dark moments that you must focus on the positives and on coming out the other side.

Round 10

WHATEVER IT TAKES

Nothing Personal

In any business, you have to leave ego at the door. I might be outspoken, and free and easy with my opinions, but I also have a reputation for being able to deal fairly with anyone. I have no problem working with people I might find problematic at some level, if it's going to benefit our fighters, our company and the sport of boxing overall.

All too often, in any negotiation, personal grudges or pure stubbornness can cloud the correct outcome. I have seen incredible deals that would benefit all parties fall apart because somebody has been insulted. In fact, I've lost count of the number of times a fight has collapsed because one boxer wants his name first on the poster.

'Yeah, but your opponent wants his on the left-hand side,' I'll point out.

'Then it's off.'

And the boxer or their team will sit there with his arms folded like a child who won't back down.

'Are you serious?' I'll say. 'There's a huge sum on the table, your legacy is at stake, and yet you're going to walk away over the difference between left and right?'

'Yes.'

Whatever your aims or ambitions, do not let the personal get in the way of the professional. It might seem like the most important issue in the world in the heat of the moment, but you have to be big enough to see beyond that.

When it comes to sitting at the negotiating table, always bring an open mind. Baggage of any kind will only get in the way. If you're in a relationship, and it doesn't end well. Maybe you feel bitter in the break-up, in which case there's every chance you carry that into the next relationship. If you haven't dealt with that emotional baggage, what hope do you have of making a success of this new one? In the world of boxing negotiation, where people regularly feel fucked over, it happens time and time again. As a result, I can sit down at the table with a seasoned promoter and find they're so bitter from decades of toxic negotiations, they've adopted a position before we've even begun.

If you enter into any kind of talks, you have to park the personal at the door. The moment you go in thinking, *Well, I don't even like this guy*, you're done. How can you possibly think smart, straight and balanced otherwise?

In my experience, dealing with people as you find them is the most effective way of getting the deal done. Even if you don't see eye-to-eye as individuals, there's an outcome to be had that benefits everyone. Once that goal is uppermost in the mind, you're over one of the greatest hurdles that lie between you and signatures on the contract.

It's natural to have a perception of the people you're dealing with. I find many people have formed an opinion of me before we've even met. Later, they might express surprise that

I turned out to be alright, and I always wonder what they expected.

It also tells me that when we first sat down, they had a strategy in place that fell apart when I didn't live up to the character in their minds. Again, what a waste of time! I once found myself facing a guy who wanted to sell his company, but changed his mind at the last minute when he learned I'd be heading it up.

'I can't do it, Eddie. Not anymore.'

I can't imagine myself in this guy's shoes. There is nothing wrong with having principles. It's important to know what you believe in. Pride is another matter, however. If you're negotiating for the greater good of your business, then fucking swallow it! Ego can be your own worst enemy. To make it worse, people often cover for poor decisions based on pride by telling themselves it's principle. Don't be the one who walks away on this basis.

Let's go back to running that marathon again. You've ticked off twenty miles and it's all looking good for the final six.

Negotiations can be simple, and they can be incredibly complicated. Sometimes talks can create more talks, or threaten to end before you've begun. When things are getting difficult, the easiest thing in the world is to walk away, or not even show up at all. Why put yourself through all the grief when you have a nice business anyway?

Because without making that effort, your business will not grow.

If it was easy, everyone would be doing it. Some times the deal feels miles off. Remember, focus on solving those little problems and keep ticking off the miles. I'm sure people will remember back in 2013, I secured a fight between Carl Froch and George Groves at the Manchester Arena. Froch was defending his unified WBA and IBF Super-Middleweight belts, with Groves as the mandatory contender for the latter. The pair taunted each other heavily in the build-up to the fight, and though Froch was the favourite, he faced a young challenger who put it right on him from the first bell.

It shaped up to be an outstanding fight, and a major shock looked likely as Groves maintained the upper hand, dropping Carl in the first round. In round nine, despite taking a serious beating, Froch put some shots together and landed a few flush on Groves, who reeled on the ropes. He certainly looked unsteady from where I was sitting, but the arena erupted when the referee wrapped his arms around Groves and stopped the fight. With opinion fiercely divided, especially between the two fighters, calls for a rematch began immediately.

As a result, I was faced with negotiating another fight in an atmosphere dripping with bad blood.

Right from the beginning, the two fighters were at war. Froch didn't like Groves. Having won the first fight, but stung by criticism that he didn't deserve it, Carl was reluctant to give him another opportunity. At the same time, Groves felt his stock had risen considerably following the first fight, and he wanted more money. Throughout, the fans and the media were clamouring for me to get the deal over the line, which piled on the pressure.

All sorts of complications kept rising up at me. At times it felt as if I was putting out one fire and watching another blaze start. Even when the whole deal looked like it would go up in flames, I never lost sight of the fact that we would stage that fight, and do so on an epic scale at Wembley Stadium; newly rebuilt and ready to host a record-breaking crowd for the time of 80,000.

Was it worth it? Absolutely. Did anyone have a clue how

difficult that deal was to pull off? None at all, and they will never know enough how tough it was. But then that's my job as the promoter. The fighters were there to settle a score and the fans to enjoy every second of what proved to be a memorable night and one of the best one-punch knockouts you're likely to see – the last punch Froch threw before heading into the sunset.

I aim to be straightforward and respectful in business, in the expectation that others extend the same to me. In boxing, however, there are no barriers to entry when it comes to working in the sport. So, if someone phones me up about a fighter they represent, and a fight they have in mind, I'll treat them seriously. That can be challenging, as it is in any business, when those players reveal themselves to have no clue or understanding of what's required of them or the financial risk at stake. Whenever you find yourself in this position, you've got to go away and do your homework, because if you come to the table unprepared, it's disrespectful and the deal is going to suffer.

Deal Breakers

Before you sit around the negotiating table, be in no doubt about what you're hoping to achieve. The outcome might be clear, and hopefully with some tough but respectful talking and flexibility from all sides, you'll achieve your goal. But what are the values that you're not prepared to concede?

Representing Matchroom, I must see two qualities in a deal before we shake hands. Firstly, is it value for money? This is not just to the company, but also to the fans out there. Secondly, does it uphold our reputation?

It's second nature for me to think in these terms. They

represent the values I grew up with, but I didn't get them all from my dad. The efforts my mum made to teach me the value of money were not lost on me, either. Dad would've been skint without her.

He was flash with the cash that he made, but strived to put on shows that fans were happy to pay to see. 'We must give value for money' has been one of his mantras for decades, and it's something that works for every business. There's no better feeling for us than when people leave an arena, or switch off their TVs, saying, 'That was worth every penny,' because that's where longevity lies. Your reputation is everything.

It doesn't matter what field you're in. If you're delivering a quality product to market, and customers feel they're getting value for money, your reputation will strengthen and allow you to evolve. It's the only way to stand the test of time. Any other strategy might make you a quick buck, but it will not last for long. Which is why it has to be hard-wired into the deals I make.

Reputation doesn't simply build a loyal customer base. For us, it plays a vital role when it comes to working with anyone from suppliers to sponsors and broadcasters. When I went into boxing with Matchroom, I knew the work my dad had done with the sport would open doors. We were known for being solid, honest, people who put on quality shows. Nobody ever complained that they hadn't been paid, or that we weren't open and honest when it came to negotiating, and that made life so much easier when I sat down to hammer out a deal. Even if people openly dislike me, or think I'm arrogant, they know hand on heart that I am always true to my word.

On a personal level, you're not going to appeal to everyone. Professionally, if you're known to be a straight shooter, those people will still want to do business with you.

Where difficulties can kick in, of course, is when the people you're dealing with don't conduct themselves to the same standard.

Eyes on the Prize

Reaching an agreement is rarely straightforward. If it was easy, everyone would be doing it, and I'm excited when faced with a deal that's proving difficult to nail down. Often that's down to one or two complexities, which is fine if the people you're dealing with are on the same page as you. Honesty goes such a long way in business. If you trust the people you're dealing with, it makes it so much easier to work towards an outcome that leaves everyone feeling like a winner.

When dealing with anyone who is proving difficult, it's rare for me to call it a day. My schooling selling double glazing taught me to keep my eyes on the prize at all times. There have been occasions when this was put to the test, and notably one case where I wasn't trying to negotiate a deal, but save a show along with the reputation of a boxer.

When you're sitting between two fighters at a press conference, you can feel the tension in the air. Even with security on hand, I'm aware that it puts me physically in the firing line should anything kick off. In the boxing world, people often mark me down as a wet lettuce. I'm not exactly from the street, after all, and my career in the ring could probably be classified as 'useless'. Even so, I'm 6 feet 4 inches and broadly built, so as long as these guys aren't coming at me, I can at least get between them.

That opportunity never arrived back in December 2016, when Dereck Chisora picked up the table he was sitting behind while we faced the media, and hurled it at his opponent,

Dillian Whyte. One minute these guys were trading insults ahead of their heavyweight clash at the Manchester Arena, the next Chisora exploded and sent the table straight at my head.

A moment of shock seized the room, before chaos broke out. Chisora was scuffling with security, throwing his weight a bit. I was up on my feet along with everyone else, thinking we were fucked. With only three days to go before the fight, after all the hard work and effort we had put into building momentum, the whole thing was thrown into jeopardy.

Boxing is a brutal, gladiatorial sport, in which emotions often run hot. It's also governed by a strict code of conduct, which Chisora had just smashed up like the table.

Naturally, the British Boxing Board of Control launched an immediate inquiry. Voices called for Chisora to be disqualified and banned from the sport, and I had a big fire on my hands. The main event for that night was Anthony Joshua's defence of his heavyweight IBF title against Éric Molina, but there was a lot of interest in this supporting fight. The pay-per-view numbers were dependent on it, and so losing Chisora/Whyte from the billing would create a major problem.

When the call came from the Board of Control, I was expecting it. This close to the show, I had assumed they would give Chisora a pending suspension and let him fight. The Board were having none of it, and insisted he attend an emergency disciplinary hearing on the Friday. This was also the day of the weigh-in, and a time when boxers are totally focused on the job at hand. It was far from ideal, but I had no other choice. I gave them my word that Chisora would attend, and I'd be there myself to argue his case.

'Dereck, this isn't going to be easy,' I said to him, in the corridor outside the room convened for the hearing. 'You need to stay calm and take the rap.'

'Yeah, but I'm not having them talk down to me.'

Inside, dozens of people awaited our appearance. Chisora is a mountain of a man, and was still wound up by the whole episode. I could see the tension literally pulsing through the veins in his neck.

'We can do this,' I told him, clapping him on the shoulder, while trying hard to hide the fact that my confidence was shot.

All talk in the room stopped as we entered. As one, everyone stared at Dereck. We took our seats beside each other, and I prayed another table wasn't set to go flying.

'Mr Chisora,' said the chair of the hearing, who began reading from a list in his hands. 'In 2013, you were alleged to have used bad language at a press conference. 2016, you spat water in Wladimir Klitschko's face . . .' The way he read this out like a rap sheet did not bode well. Beside me, Dereck began to bristle. When the chair had finished with the list, he stared across the room. 'It seems like you are trouble, no?'

'Dillian provoked me,' growled Dereck, barely audible.

'So you picked up a table,' said the chair, turning to address the room now as if to gather their support, 'and you threw it at him?'

Dereck's leg started to go up and down as he bounced on the ball of his foot. There was no doubt in my mind that at this point he wanted to to smash the room to bits and everyone in it.

'Do you know,' he said, barely concealing his fury, 'what a fighter has to go through?'

Before the chair could draw breath, I had placed my hand on Dereck's shoulder. Not that it would stop him from erupting, but I had to do something.

'With respect,' I jumped in, 'I don't think it's fair to place

Mr Chisora in this environment with just days before the fight. May I have a word in private with him outside?'

In the corridor, with the fate of the fight in my hands, I faced Dereck square on and appealed to him to think of the bigger picture.

'You have to hold it together,' I reasoned. 'Just for five minutes. All you have to do is go in there and apologise. Tell them boxing is your life and that if you don't fight tomorrow, you'll be unable to support your family. Can you do this for me, Del?'

Chisora listened to me while breathing like a bull. I stared at him, silently appealing to him. I knew the worst thing I could've done was anger him. He would've chinned me straight away. It reminded me of how I could be at school when that chip weighed heavily on my shoulder. If a teacher threatened me with detention unless I did as I was told, then I'd have just kicked off. It was only if they invited me to do something, believing that I had it in me, that I would comply.

'Alright,' Chisora said eventually, and I breathed out long and hard.

Returning to the hearing, Dereck did exactly as I had asked. He apologised, talked about the challenges he faced growing up, and the salvation and guidance he found in boxing. He was brilliant. An absolute star.

'Thank you, Dereck,' I said, taking over in case anything else triggered the red mist. 'May I let him go now, please,' I added, addressing the chair. 'Hopefully he still has a fight to prepare for.'

The committee took a while to reach their decision. I was outside in the corridor with one ear to the door. Quite a few members weren't buying it. They wanted him done. Several had been touched by his speech, however, and we won the vote to proceed by a single vote. Chisora was landed with a thirty-thousand pound fine and permitted to fight. Immediately, I called him with the good news.

'I ain't paying the fine,' he told me, but I wasn't going to let that stop us now.

Somehow, we had salvaged the fight from chaos. It had taken twenty-four hours of intense negotiating that was a far cry from any conventional business deal. Despite the differences, it still relied on understanding people and relating to them. As a result, Chisora had swallowed his considerable pride and expressed contrition for his behaviour. That had been enough to persuade the board, though I knew there were limits to how far he would go. Chisora ended up losing out to Whyte, but the fight was one of the best heavyweight fights I have ever witnessed.

Even though it was me who paid the fucking fine out of my own pocket, for the sake of the fight, it was worth every penny.

Dereck Chisora had made me a promise in that corridor, and lived up to it. Other deals are sealed with a handshake, but mostly, business demands some sort of contract or agreement. There are times when I'd prefer not to have one, simply because I am good to my word, but I understand the purpose of a piece of paper signed and enshrined by law. A contract isn't there to restrict you, but to guarantee all parties uphold an agreement. It's a security not a straight jacket.

The promoter Don King is noted as once saying, 'Negotiations begin once the contract is signed.' It's a great line and sadly so true, especially in the world of boxing. It also pisses me off that it's a reality, because it means the deal is never done. Meeting anyone honourable is such a rarity, and yet that's when solid business gets done. Usually, it's a question of agreement, handshake and signature, and then there might be doubts. And it does my head in.

A central feature in any good contract for a boxing fight is a rematch clause. When a boxer challenges a champion for the title and wins, they fight again. In many ways it means the chance for them to make yet more money, and it is a standard feature of the contract when you get to big-league boxers. By the time Anthony Joshua held all the heavyweight belts, following his victory over Joseph Parker in 2018, he had the pick of the crop to challenge him. As top dog, he could select a fighter and give them a chance to seize the crown. Should that fighter win, as was the case with Andy Ruiz Jr's shock victory in New York, then the rematch clause kicks in.

When it comes to negotiating the first fight, most boxers scramble to accept the rematch clause. Who wouldn't want a chance to unseat the champion and double your money in a second fight? The difficulties emerge should they win and their stock value rises. With people in their ear telling them they're the king of the world, the fighter looks at their contract and, all of a sudden, what looked like a dream come true on paper becomes the worst deal in the world.

'Congratulations,' I said to Ruiz Jr's advisors, shortly after he defeated AJ. 'We'll see you for the rematch.'

'Yeah, we need to talk about that,' said one of his representatives.

The response came as no surprise, but it signalled trouble ahead and when I left MSG that night I knew the negotiations had just begun. The fact that the President of Mexico flew Ruiz Jr back a national hero told me that I was probably going to encounter difficulties. Nevertheless, as I reminded his people, we had a contract that agreed he would fight Anthony Joshua again and it was solid.

'Things have changed,' one of his advisors told me when I next contacted them.

'In what way?'

'Well, he's champion.'

'Yes, I know. That's why the rematch clause is in the contract you signed.'

Faced with getting him back in the ring, it was an exchange that set the tone for what would be the most difficult negotiation of my career so far.

At Matchroom, I strive for fairness. I recognise that if a fighter wins and triggers the rematch clause, they deserve a bigger pay-out the second time around. Frankly, it's worth it to avoid this exact scenario. Even though many other promoters offer the same fee, I had in fact doubled the money for Ruiz Jr. At the time, given that he'd come to me via a message over Instagram, my offer was met with nothing but gratitude. *You've changed my life, Eddie. I can't thank you enough.* That sort of thing.

Then he wins the fight, becomes the first Mexican American world heavyweight champion, and I have made a solemn promise to AJ to bring this guy back into the ring.

Two weeks after the fight, on a much-needed holiday in Ibiza, where I was celebrating my 40th, my phone rang poolside.

'Eddie, can we discuss the rematch clause?' Ruiz Jr's advisor didn't wait for me to respond. 'Andy wants to fight, but we need to talk about the money.'

'What do you mean? The money is very clear in the contract.'

'Yes, but he's a star now.'

'That's what the rematch clause is for,' I reminded him again. 'It's for double the money and you and Andy signed the contract.'

'Yeah, but as we know,' said the guy down the line, 'contracts are there to be broken.'

As soon as he said that to me, I knew what I was facing here. From that moment on, the nice guy stuff stopped. Because now it was about principle, protecting my position, fronting it out, and ultimately keeping my promise to AJ.

In any walk of life, there will always be someone who reneges on a deal. I understand that sometimes situations change, but if it comes down to greed, that's when you have to stand your ground. You start using leverage, and talk about honour, because once you question someone's integrity, they tend to see sense. I always remember making an offer on a house, which was accepted by the owner. It was a good offer and he looked me in the eyes and shook my hand when I made it. A day later, he called me to say someone else had made a higher offer and could I match it?

'Do you remember we shook hands?' I asked him. 'Did that mean nothing to you?'

'You're right,' he said after a short pause, and that was it. That meant a lot to me.

When it comes down to it, the world is full of slags. What I mean by that is this: people will always try to fuck you over. And yet beneath it all, most people are made of the right stuff – it's just sometimes you have to question that to bring it out. With Ruiz Jr's people, it took the threat of legal action to make the rematch happen. I don't like resorting to lawyers. This level of heavy artillery is expensive and it kills your relationship, but at some point you have to take that stand.

In this instance, I had made a promise to AJ that he would have a chance to reclaim his titles. It was my job and my duty to do whatever it took to make sure that opportunity happened. It meant more to me than any amount of money we stood to make for the rematch. With principles at stake here, I could not let him down.

Eventually, after weeks of wrangling, our lawyers in New York issued a writ. It compelled Ruiz Jr to honour the terms of the contract or face court action. At the same time, I faced the issue of where to stage the fight, and I realised that the negotiations had only just begun.

A Contract with Greatness

This was one marathon where the markers kept coming at me. It's here that all the qualities we've discussed come into play. You've got to be at the top of your game with no cracks in your positivity, mindset, vision and drive. As soon as you start thinking it's impossible, you're done. It's not uncommon in any business venture, and demands a level head and bullet-proof commitment to getting it over the line.

We had two venues lined up for the rematch: a return to Madison Square Garden or the Millennium Stadium in Wales. AJ wanted to go back and right the wrong in America, while his training team favoured Cardiff. They sat him down and asked why the fuck he would want to fight on Ruiz Jr's home turf, and AJ said because it seemed like the right thing to do.

'That's very honourable, but let's be smart here,' I said. 'You boxed him in his country last time round. Let's get home advantage, and win these belts back.'

With AJ on board, and because the rematch clause allowed me to determine where the fight would be staged, I informed Ruiz Jr's people. The next thing I knew, Andy had gone to the media to state how unfair it would be on him to fight in AJ's backyard.

Around the same time, as I sat with my head in my hands, I received a message on Instagram. A lot of people contact me this way, but Ruiz was the only one to do so that led to a World Heavyweight Title fight. In this case, it was from a representative of Prince Khalid bin Salman bin Abdulaziz Al Saud, a member of the Saudi Arabian royal family. I'd never heard of the guy, but he was interested in talking to me about hosting a major boxing match in the Kingdom.

Previously, I'd had plenty of approaches like this from the Middle East. The proposals were always interesting and the people warm and cordial, but they'd come to nothing. There were too many agents involved, which made it hard to know what was serious. So, in my personal experience, it was a waste of time. I replied, and said I was busy focusing on bringing the Joshua/Ruiz Jr fight to Cardiff.

Shortly afterwards, I received another message asking if Prince Khalid himself could call me. Curious now, but still on guard, I gave the guy my number. I didn't really expect him to ring. I was so busy trying to work my way through the obstacles thrown up by Ruiz Jr and his team that when he did call, I wasn't in the mood to fuck around.

'I don't want to be disrespectful,' I said, 'but do you have any idea how much time I've wasted discussing fights in the Middle East?'

'But we really want to host the Anthony Joshua fight,' he said.

'Listen,' I replied, 'we've taken trips out there and even drafted contracts, but nothing ever happens.'

The prince proved himself to be a patient man, because I was quite rude to him and he persevered.

'Can you at least tell me how much it would cost to host it?'

I gave him a number, which I knew would get it done.

'That's it,' I said, thinking the end of the call was imminent.

'We're in,' said the prince.

I was certainly surprised, but my guard was still high. I didn't have the time to be messed around. So, thinking on my feet, I made him a proposal.

'I'm going to send you a contract,' I said. 'It's one we drafted for a fight in Dubai that came to nothing, but it's completely fair and covers everything for a show in the Middle East. If you're happy with this contract, and the fee we've just agreed, then you've got the fight. But if you want a single change, then no deal.'

I gave him forty-eight hours, and figured I'd never hear from him again.

Twenty-four hours later, a lawyer representing Prince Khalid emailed me with dozens of amendments to the contract. I decided to ring the prince directly.

'I don't mean to be disrespectful,' I said, 'but I haven't got time to renegotiate a deal. Let's just leave it.'

'We'll sign it as it is,' he said.

At this point, I hadn't talked to AJ about any of this, simply because I didn't want to mess him around. When the contract finally came through, signed without amendment, I made that call. As I explained it to Anthony, the Saudi offer could be the venue that would solve the puzzle. Ruiz Jr didn't want to fight in Wales and AJ's training team had agreed that New York was out for him. This would be a neutral venue, I explained. It would be a new market for him, and with a bigger financial return.

AJ is a fighter who likes to have all the facts. He's smart, he listens and likes to think. At his level of boxing, in effect he also owns the pot that pays for the show. This covers everything, including the other boxer's fee and my percentage. It makes everything so much more transparent, and works well for all involved. It also meant the final decision rested with Anthony.

When he agreed in principle, my next step was to make sure the money promised by the prince actually materialised. It was all part of the process that meant the boxers were ticked. We couldn't go to Ruiz Jr's people with the Saudi proposal, only to discover it was hot air. According to the terms of the contract, the prince had agreed to pay one third of the fee up front within five days of signing. We set up an escrow account, and made regular calls to my bank for an update. We were due an eight-figure sum. It was not insignificant. With nothing incoming from Saudi Arabia, I called Prince Khalid.

'I'll be straight with you,' I said tersely, 'if the money isn't in the account by the agreed date, then the deal is off.'

'It's coming, it's been sent,' the prince insisted.

I'll be honest, I didn't believe him. I began to blame myself for being drawn in, until I called the bank before the close of play on the final day and they confirmed the money was there. When the prince heard from me a few minutes later, calling like his long-lost son, he laughed.

'You didn't believe me, did you?' he said.

With the fight confirmed for Saudi Arabia, my next step was to get Andy Ruiz Jr on board and fast. Why? Because if word got out to the media first, he could still cause me problems. I called his people, reminding them that they had been insisting on a neutral venue, and presented them with exactly that.

Now, Saudi Arabia as a venue for a heavyweight boxing match comes with a particular set of problems. I was well aware of the controversies of the country, and talked it through with Ruiz Jr's people as I had with AJ. We knew there would be controversy, but my view was that these fighters were prepared to put their lives on the line when they climbed into the ring. What right did anyone have to stop them from doing that for the biggest purse on offer?

In context, and having discussed the wider issue at length with Prince Khalid, my advice to them both was to recognise this was the best deal on the table: a neutral venue, a big return, a new market and a host committed to showing the world that the Kingdom was undergoing a process of modernisation.

On top of that, despite the legal threats, I still had Ruiz Jr wriggling to get off the hook. As world champion, he could have chosen that moment to retire and we would've been fucked. The temptation would've been there for him. Why risk going into the ring when you can hang up your gloves with the crown? In terms of talking to Andy and his people, I had to tread carefully and address his rightful concerns about my proposal.

Eventually, after a marathon with so many twists and turns, which included compromise on both sides, we had a deal. The Clash on the Dunes was announced for December 2019. The scale of the undertaking was immense. At the time, with three months before the fight, the venue was basically desert land in Diriyah, just outside the Saudi capital, Riyadh. It was also a controversial choice in many circles, but I was ready for anything. I had made a promise to AJ that I would give him this chance to reclaim his belts, and under the best possible circumstances.

With the negotiations behind us, it was time to do what Matchroom did best, and stage a show that would go down in boxing history. I did not waver in my belief that we could achieve this, no matter what obstacles lay ahead, because I knew we possessed that one element all businesses need to succeed – a drive and energy that could be summed up in one word: relentless. The event was spectacular and I met a man in Prince Khaled who kept his word every step of the way.

ROUND 10 – KEY TAKEAWAYS

- In any business, you have to leave ego at the door. All too often, in any negotiation, personal grudges or pure stubbornness can cloud the correct outcome. I have seen incredible deals that would benefit all parties fall apart because of a personal grudge or jagged emotions.

- Reaching an agreement is rarely straightforward. If it was easy, everyone would be doing it, and I'm excited when faced with a deal that's proving difficult to nail down. Often that is down to complexities, which is fine if the people you're dealing with are on the same page as you. Honesty goes such a long way in business, but as Warren Buffett once said, 'Honesty is a very expensive gift, don't expect it from cheap people.'

- You've got to be at the top of your game, with no cracks in your positivity, mindset, vision and drive. As soon as you start thinking something's impossible, you're done. You must start seeing the opportunities rather than the obstacles. It's not uncommon to face problems in any business venture and it will always demand a level head and bullet-proof commitment. It takes the same energy to worry as it does to be positive, so why not use it to focus on the goal.

Round 11

RELENTLESS

If you want to be successful, you need to accept some hard truths. The fact is it demands the kind of sacrifices that are going to make you unpopular at home, and at times perhaps, the person you shouldn't be.

On the domestic front, if you want to be a model partner, then you need another job. Probably my greatest sacrifice over the last decade has been the time I've had to spend away from my family. It isn't only the time I've missed with the kids as they've grown up, but after a demanding work trip, I can be tired, ratty, and sometimes all that's on my mind is business. It's an obsession and I won't let the game beat me.

At the same time, over the years I've come to realise that there is a fine line between being relentless and being an arsehole.

It's very easy to get lost in the hustle, but the truth is that happiness is everything. There's no doubt that a balanced personal life will always give you a balanced mind to make the right decisions. I have no problem being outclassed, but I will not accept being outworked, and if I really want something, I will go out and get it. If that means pushing hard, then I follow my dad's advice to 'get up an hour earlier and go to bed an hour later'. It's something that has stuck with me, because there is truth in it.

Even so, there will be days when you feel that you're at a dead end despite the hard work. Just aim to see beyond that. Ultimately, the will to win and the desire to succeed are key to unlocking your potential.

Failure Is Unacceptable

In business and life, you have to accept that you can't win every time. This doesn't sit well with me and it never has done. I recognise there is truth in it, but prefer to look at it like this: whatever you set your sights on achieving, you can *never* go in thinking you might fail. Every time I make a bold move, failure never comes into my mind. I'm aware what the potential problems are and what could fail – it's a case of feeling the fear and doing it anyway.

I know the parenting manual says that what matters is the taking part and not the winning, but let's get real here. In business, you don't make sacrifices so people can say, 'Well, he did his best.' It's meaningless, and amounts to nothing. All I can ever do is give 110 per cent. And if I make that commitment, refusing to be outworked in the process, but I still don't win – then, that amounts to nothing more than failure.

If there's one thing that I want you to take away from this book, it's this: do not be outworked. If you want success, you've got to put your head down and hustle. Simple as that. In order to be successful, you have to be willing to put in the work.

Part of maintaining a winning outlook is knowing how to manage those times when things don't work out. It should be painful if you've gone all out to achieve your goal and then fallen short. If you look back and think you could have done better if you'd worked a bit harder, then you deserved to fail. I'm talking about those times when you've put your heart and soul into a project that doesn't pay off for reasons beyond your control.

No matter how much it hurts, that feeling doesn't last if you can learn from the experience. This way, you won't look back with regrets. It's a question of finding strength through failure, and from that comes a mental stability. There's no way you can go full tilt into future projects if you're eaten up by the last one. There has to be acceptance, but that can only come through learning hard lessons.

If failure is unacceptable to me, then by extension winning is everything. Some people might think this is a brutal outlook, but it's central to my welfare. The focus and drive required puts me in a great place mentally. I'm fulfilled by the challenge of meeting a target, because to me results are everything.

When valuing a company, nobody disregards poor results and credits them for working hard. That's not how business operates. You are judged by the targets you hit, but only you can determine what should be considered a success. Whether you're shooting for a seven-figure turnover or simply hoping to break even in challenging conditions, success means different things to people at different times. What matters is that you have a clear understanding of what success means to you.

It's not always about money, of course. Maybe your goal is simply to provide a quality product, or delivering a service that makes a difference in the community. That's your call. What matters is your perception of success, because that's where you'll find fulfilment.

The Courage of Conviction

In 2014, five years before we announced a major boxing match in Saudi, I looked out from the players' entrance to Wembley Stadium and knew I had to stage a show here. I had been touring football clubs, looking for a venue for the rematch between George Groves and Carl Froch. Following Groves' shock defeat against Froch, the clamour among fans to see them clash again was huge. We hadn't done big numbers for the first show, even though it was a magnificent fight, but I sensed this one would be huge.

'It has to be here,' I told my dad on the phone. I was looking up and around at the national stadium's tiered seating.

'Wembley takes ninety thousand,' said Bazza, who had seen under half that number come to his biggest fight between Nigel Benn and Chris Eubank at Old Trafford. 'Don't be daft.'

'We're going to sell out,' I said. 'Trust me.'

It's easy to get carried away with a big idea in business. That's why it's so important to understand your market and have absolute trust in your convictions. Ever since the first Froch/Groves fight, when the referee arguably stepped in too early, the chat on social media had been deafening. The decision to award the fight to Froch had left fans desperate to see the pair in the ring again. I had only to scroll through Twitter mentions to be certain that I could be the first boxing promoter to stage a show at the newly rebuilt stadium.

It didn't feel like a risk in any way. If anything, as a fan myself, I would've been first in the queue for tickets. It was that pure passion that convinced me this was the ideal venue. I lost no sleep about it, and devoted myself to selling the narrative, fuelling excitement and ensuring I could deliver on the promise of an epic fight.

Sure enough, when the show was announced and tickets went on sale, we sold 80,000 tickets in the first day.

Every business player needs courage in their convictions. The absolute certainty that you're on the right path is essential for momentum when the going gets tough. I certainly anticipated a bumpy ride when we announced that AJ would be fighting Ruiz in Saudi. It wasn't only the strong opinion that would be stirred up about hosting a fight in the Kingdom. All I could do was place my trust in Prince Khalid when he promised to host a show that exceeded all expectation. I had nothing but his word to go on.

In September, two months before the fight, we flew out for a site visit and found only levelled ground. We went back a month later. They'd added a few seats and a small stand. Prince Khalid assured me it would be ready. I had to trust him and focus on all the other moving parts.

So, what was behind my conviction that I'd made the right call for the rematch? I take people as I find them, Prince Khalid was nothing but honest, enthusiastic and courteous in my dealings with him. In the four weeks left before the fight, he was true to his word and created a phenomenal arena. As for the stick I received about staging the fight in the desert, I did my homework. I recognised the issues around the controversies, but there was also an underlying investment from the Saudis to bring in world-class sport and entertainment. The PGA tour had added the country to the calendar, as had WWE, while Formula E had recently raced around the streets of Riyadh.

With this spotlight on the Kingdom, I wasn't alone in seeing the potential for change. Above all, however, I was focused on staging a fight there and doing the very best for the boxers. If I bowed to pressure about where they should fight, and removed the best opportunity they had for maximum return, I wouldn't be doing my job as a promoter. At any time, my role is to help these boxers get the best deal that they can, create a legacy, and then get out of the sport safely. That is the brutal reality of boxing.

I knew I could get the fight made. I was also well aware that I would face a huge amount of criticism, even though every other promoter in the world had been trying their nuts off to stage a show there. In this instance, my integrity was pinned to doing the right thing for the fighters, and so I could hold my head high. I had no second thoughts. My conviction did not waver.

Nor did I sit back for one moment in the build-up to that fight. Even when everything has fallen into place, there is never room in any business for complacency. At times I would face a dozen interviewers at once, with questions I've never had to answer before. I met them head on, spoke form the heart and basic honesty.

In life and business, you have to be willing to be brave, jump in and take risks. Without risk, there is no reward. It's that easy. If you're going to make a big decision, you have to back yourself one hundred per cent and believe in yourself. If you start second-guessing, it's game over. It's not going to work out. Commit yourself fully to something and pursue your goals with a relentless attitude.

Confidence Not Complacency

When we talk about aims and ambitions, or a measure of success, levels often come into play. We place ourselves at a certain rung on the ladder and look up. It's human nature. In business, some might set their sights on a certain level, and relax when they reach it. Through my eyes, it's simply another mile marker.

We are a wealthy family. We've worked hard, and got a few

quid. We featured in the *Sunday Times* Rich List recently. Curious, I found myself going up through the list where people sat on billions of pounds. How did they do that, I asked myself? How on earth do you accumulate that kind of wealth? It made me think about what I need to do with my own work, but not out of jealousy. I want to create opportunities that allow me to make that journey to the next level, because I love what I do.

It's a great mindset to have in business. Quite simply, it means there are no limits. It's also very hard to go back. Think of how it is when we fly. I spent years flying to the States in economy and almost immediately start thinking about upgrading to premium economy. Once you're there, business is down the aisle. So you work a bit harder for the privilege, and then there you are with your legs stretched out thinking this is the bollocks. Then you arrive at the airport one day and they offer you the chance to go first class. Next thing you know, you're in the lap of luxury, thinking, *Well, business was shit!* From there, it's only a matter of time before you come across someone with a private jet, and so it goes on. In life, there is always another level.

So, if you're like me, then don't get hung up on long-term goals. You might work a lifetime to achieve that dream in your head, but once you reach it, you'll only be focused on pursuing the next one. Don't be single minded not to enjoy the rise through the levels, but always remember there is more to overcome.

Going back to that marathon metaphor, if you're working hard at going the distance, you have to fight off the desire to have a rest. It's easily done. The moment you look back at how far you've come and think, *Fuck it, I'll have a little walk*, this is when people overtake you.

In business, you simply can't afford to be complacent. It can kick in for all sorts of reasons. Maybe you've worked hard for your success. Perhaps you've built yourself an empire and that same hunger you started with no longer exists. Well, congratulations, but unless you keep a sharp eye open, someone will come along to try claiming it for themselves. When things are going well, my dad is always quick to give me a reality check. 'Don't get carried away with yourself,' he'll warn me, and he's right. Because if you think you've become untouchable, and assume things will continue to go right automatically, then your drive drops away and the quality of your work will slip.

No matter what success you've achieved in your life, if you're still hungry for it, then age is no excuse to sit back. We all mellow in some respects, and hopefully grow wiser, but if you look at my old man, he's still as driven as he was forty years ago. That's just how he is. As time ticks by, I'm keenly aware that I need to keep in touch with my audience. There are new generations of boxing fans constantly coming through. I need to connect with these people and bring them the sport in a way that's going to guarantee their engagement.

When I first started out, I looked at the promoters who had done well for themselves, but nobody was going to the shows they were putting on in sports halls and leisure centres. They'd become complacent, whereas I had the hunger and drive to shake things up. With this in mind, I made the bold move to promote YouTube star KSI. In 2018, KSI took an online dispute with a fellow YouTuber, Joe Weller, and settled it in a boxing match at the Copper Box Arena in London. The pair were both amateurs, but KSI's passion shone through and his audience loved it.

Fired up by his victory, he took things to the next level by fighting the American social media star Logan Paul. The fight sold out 21,000 tickets at Manchester Arena. It was an impressive number, but nothing compared to the phenomenal demand to watch that fight live on YouTube.

These fans were kids who had no other interest in boxing beyond their two heroes, and they lapped it up. It tore up the traditional platform model, showed me how the world was changing in some respects, and that seized my attention. Yes, I could've sat back and dismissed it as a novelty fight, but I didn't want to see someone else do this. When I took on the rematch, which was staged in LA in November 2019, I knew I'd get stick from the hardcore fans. This was around the same time as the Saudi build-up, but the abuse I got for this one knocked that out of the water.

Then again, I wasn't looking at KSI or Logan Paul thinking they were great fighters. They turned professional for the fight, and all credit to them both for putting in the work to achieve that, but this was always about reaching an entirely new audience for me. So, I asked myself if this was right for the business, and for my broadcasters, and the answer was 100 per cent yes.

People suggested I was selling out putting on this fight, but my vision was different. I wasn't selling out for money. I was promoting two global stars who might not have been the best fighters, but were getting in the ring. This was opening up a new market for me. These were young, tech-savvy sports fans, and I had the opportunity to introduce them to the world of boxing. They don't watch the BBC or traditional outlets. The way of digesting content is changing, and I had the perfect partner to deliver this in DAZN.

I can also say that KSI and Logan Paul are geniuses. They're not idiots who make videos. They have a brilliant understanding of their audience. Ahead of the first press conference – at which three thousand people had turned up and which four million would go on to watch online – I went into KSI's dressing room to explain how it all worked.

'So, I'll do my thing and then pass it over to you,' I finished.

KSI looked at me as if I'd spelled out the obvious.

'We're good,' he said. 'We know what we're doing.'

After that I went to see Logan Paul and he said exactly the same thing.

These guys knew exactly what was required of them. They're showmen, natural storytellers at heart, and they know how to deliver it. They were prepared to document every moment of their preparation for the fight and serve it up in ways that could be consumed, shared and spread around the globe. As I had the opportunity to put young fighters on the undercard, that meant we also had an opportunity to introduce new fans to the sport.

For all the criticism, that fight connected me to a younger generation. I don't pretend totally to understand that audience, but the experience gave me a better understanding. It's a work in progress that ultimately will benefit the sport. How? If even a small percentage of that huge global audience who followed the KSI/Logan Paul fight saga go on to become tomorrow's hardcore boxing fans, it makes it worthwhile for me. I was thirty when I first started in boxing. I was a fan, I still am, but I'm not *that* audience. Even though I'm older, I need to forge that connection.

That's where my predecessors went wrong, really, and the reason why my critics were looking at two YouTubers and saying, 'What is this shit? They're just kids!' Yes, they were young, but at that press conference an entire generation was watching. If I didn't reach out, my audience would simply grow old with me, and we'd all fade away. I'm not having that because it's important to be open to new ideas. If you keep doing things the same way, you'll keep getting the same results. Being open-minded allows you to pivot quickly and identify new opportunities. I could've been arrogant, rested on my achievements and sneered at these two YouTubers, but that's not in my nature. Social media didn't merely have a role in that fight – it pretty much played out on mobile screens from the press conference onwards. It also meant my face became familiar to kids outside of boxing circles, which no doubt helped the parody account 'No Context Hearn' take off. I look at all these short clips of me circling around and find it funny. There is one in particular where I say, 'The backlash makes me horny,' which was in response to the grief I was getting for staging that fight in the first place.

My view was that people who dismissed it as a novelty show lacked vision. And if they lacked vision, they didn't love the sport as I did. I wanted to see boxing continue to grow, and if that meant people knocking me, I would work even harder to prove to them that this was exactly how to make it thrive. I'm also well aware that No Context raises awareness of my work as much as a smile, and I'm happy with that on both counts.

The more I put myself out there, attracting interest in boxing, the further I am away from saying, 'Do you know what? I've made it,' because with passion comes ambition and I've only just begun.

There is a fine line between ambition and greed, of course, but I don't look at it that way. Every business player wants to make as much money as possible. That's the name of the game, but it should never be the sole focus. At Matchroom, when we set our business targets at the start of the year, the actual figure is irrelevant. We don't come up with a number because we want to buy a plane. It exists as a focus to improve the company.

Whether we're talking a thousand pounds or one hundred million, the relentless charge to meeting that target should be about the health of your business, not your bank account. I do think you have to be careful here, as it's all too easy to lose sight of the passion and become focused entirely on money and power. I see it happen all the time, and it doesn't bring out the best in people. Nor is it a sign of success. It's an addiction that will never bring happiness.

Happiness Head On

Take anyone with a regular job. They wake up at the same time in the morning, have breakfast with the kids, and then go to work. Those eight hours might feel like a grind, but afterwards they can walk away and literally switch off. The rest of the day belongs to them, and I envy that life in a way.

At the same time, I can't imagine myself in those shoes.

It's sad, in a way, that in my professional life I'm rarely content with anything I've delivered. I'm a very happy family man. Together with my wife, I love encouraging the kids to grow up with good manners and values. That's all fine, but I've had to make sacrifices at home in order to pursue success at work. It's part of the job description in some ways. If I wasn't making sacrifices, then it would be impossible to be where I am. Fundamentally, the only way you can be more successful than other people is by putting in the most work.

From stock market traders who get up at 4 a.m. to deal on an overseas exchange, to the boxer training nonstop, sacrifice is a compulsory requirement on the road to success. You must be relentless. I understand this, and embrace it, because all I want to do is keep building a legacy my dad started from nothing. You have to find your reason for doing something. What's your motivation? Once you have this, you won't be outworked.

Obviously, I do have to be careful, however, because I don't want to look back and say to myself, 'Fuck, you were never really happy, despite all the things you achieved.' Like so many things in life, it's a work in progress for me. It's important to keep this in mind when you set out on your journey.

Happiness and success can be the same thing, but first you have to establish what success means through your eyes. For me, if I'm chasing a bold target and I achieve it, that's both a success and it makes me happy. If I fail to hit that target, however, I'll be miserable. In many ways my happiness is pinned closely to realising my ambitions, but so much depends on your attitude and outlook. I can hit a number and feel good about it, but at the same time I'm sizing up the next number. It's endless for me, but I'm also passionate about the business. So, even when things are challenging, that passion contributes greatly to my wellbeing.

There is a saying that if you love what you do, then you'll never work a day in your life, and I believe there is a great deal of truth in that.

As a boxing promoter, I'm lucky enough to work with a lot of fighters I consider to be an inspiration. Like me, they are passionate about what they do. In my mind, that's where I find happiness. It's that commitment to being the best in a field that I love, even though I constantly feel there is work to be done.

Katie Taylor is an Irish boxer who embodies this mindset. She's devoted to the sport, and also to God, and as a result her life is very simple. At the forefront of women's boxing, which I believe is set to enter a golden age, Katie shuns the limelight to live and train in Connecticut, USA. She has a little apartment very close to her gym, which is basic to say the least, but that's all she wants. I admire the simplicity of this approach so much. Katie has a really peaceful frame of mind. She's following a path that has been given to her in accordance with her faith, and vows to do her best at all times with what she's been given. Only she can say what happiness means to her, but without doubt there is a contentment in her existence that serves as an example to us all.

Then there's Anthony Joshua.

I've represented AJ throughout his entire professional career. In that time, we've also become very good friends. We share the same commitment to working harder than our rivals. When we set ourselves a target, we allow nothing to get in the way. I admire him hugely. Genuinely, Anthony is a really nice guy. He lights up any room and I love being around him.

I've also seen him face up to a setback that could have crushed lesser fighters.

His came as a huge shock. He went into that fight as he always does: with the absolute confidence that he had done all the work. As it turned out, it wasn't enough. Despite all the sacrifices he'd made, aligning his whole life around that fight, he lost. Everything he had worked so hard towards came crashing down around him.

AJ being the man that he is, he handled that defeat with incredible grace. He congratulated Ruiz Jr, and blamed nobody but himself. *I have to be better*, he kept saying, to himself as much as to me, and I knew that he could do it. I also believed that if he was anything like me, then working towards reclaiming those belts would be the only way he'd be happy.

'I'm excited,' I told him after the fight. 'Going into that ring, you were the man. You had all the titles and it was all easy. You were the greatest, selling out stadiums, but now after one crazy night it's all gone. You're not the champ any more,' I said to finish. 'So, what are you going to do about it?'

AJ didn't need to reply. This was a man suffering the intense pain of losing. Rather than allow it to eat him up, I knew he would convert it into an energy. Following our return home, for every moment of each day over the months that followed, Anthony used that pain to train harder than ever before. As I've said before, setbacks pave the way for comebacks. It's how you face them that will pave the way to success. You have to be relentless in your pursuit of becoming the best. AJ's a perfectionist, which is the only way to achieve true greatness. My part of the bargain was to secure the rematch with Ruiz Jr, which drove me in different ways, but it led us to a showdown in Saudi.

We arrived with momentum behind us. I had done my homework. I knew that questions would be asked about staging a fight in a country with a controversial human rights record. I also believed that a major event such as this could be a force for good in terms of shining a light on the country and opening it up to scrutiny. Ultimately, as I said at the opening press conference, I was serving the best interests of the fighters. When it finished, I was invited into a side room so journalists could interview me on a one-to-one basis and at a greater length. As I sat down, I noticed quite a few faces who wouldn't normally show up for an AJ fight. These were news journalists, hungry for the story.

'Why are you here?' one national TV news reporter asked.

My strategy, I had decided, was to deal with this issue head on.

'Why are *you* here?' I asked in reply, and argued that there were more constructive ways of addressing the wider issues than singling out one event or company, when so many were doing business in the Kingdom. When I pointed out that included the news agency who had sent her to grill me, which made them equally complicit in the 'sportswash' she was so keen to level at me, she cut the interview.

Honesty and a smile will always stop them in their tracks. It's a fight and I gave them a reason for being here. It's a neutral venue that allowed me to get both fighters in the ring, for which they're being paid handsomely to put their lives on the line. End of story.

Come fight night, it was so unusual to see AJ first out for the ring walk. He'd been champion for so long, which gave him first choice on everything from the placement of his name on the poster to the choice of dressing room. Now that privilege belonged to Ruiz Jr, and naturally as the defending champion, he chose to come out second.

For an opponent, having to stand for longer in the ring as the champ makes his entrance can be a psychological disadvantage. No fighter wants to wait around as all eyes are on their rival. That night, however, waiting for the Mexican American, Anthony Joshua looked *reborn*.

I have never seen such a reversal of fortune take place over the space of two fights. Where Anthony had begun as the king, now he had lost that crown. At the same time, he had found that all-consuming hunger to reclaim it. As the challenger once more, he was possessed. All the little championship benefits that Ruiz Jr enjoyed simply fed into AJ's commitment to right a wrong. It energised him. Who knows whether he was happy, but in the moments before that first bell, having done all the work, it was quite clear to me that AJ had made peace with himself.

And the fight was a masterclass in redemption.

Right from the start, AJ asserted his skill. He boxed with poise and skill, which shook Ruiz Jr. The defending champion fought hard over the full twelve rounds, but AJ had it covered to win back his WBA, IBF, IBO and WBO belts.

Afterwards, addressing the crowd from the ring and the

viewers at home, the two-time world heavyweight champion thanked God for this moment, and displayed the same humility and grace as he had in defeat. It was humbling to be a part of that experience, and the joy in his eyes made it all worthwhile.

The celebrations back in the changing room were immense, but for AJ it wasn't about the fact that he had reached his goal. He was thinking, *What's next? How do I improve?* That is the mentality I share with him. We were overjoyed at the win, but now it was onto bigger and better things. That's what makes me feel alive. It's a relentless tilt towards greatness that brings me happiness. I want to help AJ to create an untouchable legacy in boxing. It's a story without end, but an honour to be a part of it. I live and breathe for this opportunity, as does everyone at Matchroom, and Anthony knows that we work ourselves to the bone to make it a success.

He's also the sort of kind-hearted guy who would give me a day off in lieu, but I'm never going to ask him for it.

ROUND 11 – KEY TAKEAWAYS

- If you want to be successful, you need to accept some hard truths. The fact is that it demands the kind of sacrifices that are going to make you unpopular indoors, and at times perhaps not a very nice person.

- It's very easy to get lost in the hustle, but the truth is that happiness is everything, so don't neglect it. There's no doubt that a balanced personal life will give you a balanced mind to make the right decisions. You will never be truly satisfied by your work until you are truly satisfied with your life.

- You are judged by the targets you hit, but only you can determine what should be considered a success. Whether you're shooting for a seven-figure turnover or simply hoping to break even in challenging conditions, success means different things to people at different times. What matters is that you have a clear understanding of what success means to you. It's not always about money, of course. Define success in your own terms and achieve it by your own rules and build the life you are proud to lead. Don't focus on others: all that matters is your own personal perception of success, because that's where you'll find fulfilment.

Round 12

WE GO AGAIN

In my career, I've never paused for breath. It's always been full on, and I thrive on that. I like to operate with energy and momentum as much as passion and commitment. With the right strategy, it all comes together as a driver for success. But I cannot take my foot off the gas.

At the same time, when you're travelling at high speed and full of adrenalin, it's easy to let moments pass you by. Ever since I started out, I've never really soaked up an achievement, because my focus is always on the next chapter.

Inevitably, there will be moments in any business career when that ride can't stay in top gear. We've dealt with setbacks, and seen how fighters turn a defeat into an energy to be better, but what happens when the road ahead changes so dramatically that all traffic grinds to a halt? Then, it's not a question of stripping down the engine and rebuilding it. It could be a question of completely redesigning the vehicle to adapt to the new conditions – and even get a head start on everyone else.

Into Lockdown

In 2020, the world as we knew it went on hold.

The coronavirus pandemic has affected our lives in ways we could never have imagined. It has changed everything, not only in our personal lives but the way we do business. There is no escape from it for companies of any shape or size. But from here on out, what will define us all is our response to the crisis.

A few weeks before things got serious, and the lockdown came into play across the UK, Matchroom had an international plan in place. We had rolled out a strategy to expand into a number of territories such as Australia, Canada, Germany and across Scandinavia. I was holding meetings all over the place, while also driving preparations for the big fights that marked the calendar for the next five months.

When Italy shut down, early in March, it forced us to cancel a show in Verona. We'd already decided to pull a fight in Milan a month earlier, when things weren't looking good there. It was then I began to pay close attention to expert forecasts, and the possibility that the virus could spread. Like any good business owner, you have to look ahead. If something is going on in the world, you need to ask what it could mean for your company. It's just good practice. In this case, it meant questioning whether three standout fights we had lined up would go ahead.

Within a very short space of time, it became apparent that the UK had not escaped the pandemic. As restrictions came into place, we were forced to cancel Anthony Joshua's mandatory against Kubrat Pulev at Tottenham Hotspur's stadium, the much-anticipated clash between Dereck Chisora and Oleksandr Usyk at the O2 in London, and Dillian Whyte v Alexander Povetkin at Manchester Arena. These were huge dates in our calendar, with tickets and pay-per-view figures selling strongly, but the situation was out of our hands. We took the hit, as did almost every company across the country at that time in some shape or form.

This sudden turn in world events presented a critical question. Like all business players, I needed to ask myself whether our company was sufficiently proofed against disaster. Had this pandemic occurred ten years earlier, Matchroom might've been in trouble. In that time, however, we'd built a solid foundation. We had strong liquidity and cash reserves to help us ride out the waves. This was our 'fuck off' money, as I like to call it, which is hard to acquire but insulated against a shock of this size. It didn't mean I could afford to be complacent, of course.

Yes, we had a strong ship, but we were sailing into a storm with no end in sight. From the biggest multinational to the homespun start-up, businesses everywhere faced an uncertain future. But that didn't make us helpless.

There are two restaurants near to where I live that stand across the road from each other. The morning after the Prime Minister announced the lockdown was in place, one of them closed until further notice. Inside, the tables had been set for that evening's service, and left in place. Quite literally, it looked like the business had been frozen in time. Overnight, this profitable venture that was regularly filled with diners had cut off all means of earning an income.

Across the road, a very different story was about to play out.

Crisis Management

In the pursuit of success, you have to be prepared to deal with bleak times. If you simply freeze, panic-stricken, you won't merely miss your immediate targets. You could well fold.

At Matchroom, with lockdown in place, we quickly went into an assessment phase. We read all our insurance policies and contracts to confirm our position. With hundreds of hotel rooms booked at any one time, for example, we got on the phones and talked to our account managers. As loyal customers, spending millions of pounds over the years, what deal could we strike to avoid cancellations in the interests of both parties? In effect, we struck compromises and deals where we could, in a bid to minimise the damage done. It was about lining up the problems we suddenly faced and ticking them off one by one. Our reaction time was critical. As with any good crisis management strategy, this was a moment to get proactive and not simply wait for people to contact us.

Perhaps most important of all, however, we had a duty to communicate with our customers and fighters.

Every business has a relationship with the people it relies on for an income. When a disruption happens, it's only natural that your customer wants to know how it's affecting things. If they've actually invested money with you, such as buying advance tickets for a show, that makes the demand for information even more pressing.

So, the worst thing you can do as a business is to go quiet. It creates anxiety and distrust, and you lose all the qualities of a vital bond. At Matchroom, we've always prided ourselves on the dialogue we have with the fans. We're across all social media platforms, and not simply as a mouthpiece to announce new shows. We engage with the fans. In many ways, as we share their passion for the sport, we are fans ourselves. This willingness and enthusiasm to talk has put us in a great position over the years. You can reach out to me personally on social media and there's a very good chance I'll reply.

So, in a time of uncertainty – especially when money is tight – people want to know what's happening. If they've shelled out for a ticket and the show has been cancelled, you have to be up front about it. The last thing you want to do is run away from the problem. It's a basic fundamental – even if you don't have any instant answers, make yourself available. Don't hide, because then people assume the worst. At the same time, other business people will be finding ways to overcome the issues you all face, and it's going to put you at the back of the queue later on. In our case, we'd cancelled shows but had every intention of restaging them. We wanted to keep our customers for when we were in a position to reschedule.

At heart, we're talking about goodwill and loyalty. In both cases, honesty is key. So, as the health crisis deepened, I wasn't only announcing cancellations. I was making myself available as Eddie, and being completely up front with people:

We've had to cancel due to events that are out of our hands. We're as gutted as you guys, but we're working hard to find a solution. We will reschedule, and as soon as the dates are confirmed, you'll be the first to know. If you would like a refund then of course we will provide that, but your tickets are valid for the show when it happens, and I've got to tell you what a fight it's going to be. Both boxers are continuing to train and they will be ready to put on a night you will never forget . . .

It goes back to pure selling in so many ways. We'd done the deal on the tickets, but now I had to sell the excitement. *Yes, there is a delay, but I guarantee the wait will be worth it. We'll add some extra fights to make up for the wait. It's going to be an incredible night!*

This wasn't an empty promise. I vowed to myself, as much as the fans, that when we came back we'd be stronger than ever before. It's the only way to ask the customer to have faith, because unless I delivered on my word, I'd lose that goodwill and loyalty in a heartbeat.

In any business, the customer needs to know you're solid, you don't bullshit and you're on hand to provide answers. The worst thing you can do is create an information vacuum. If you go silent, uncertainty will lead quickly to resentment. All the good work you might have put into your business will evaporate.

Even if you don't know the answer to a question, for example the date for a rescheduled show, be up front about that. Bring them on the journey with you. Reassure your customer base that you are working hard to create a solution, and going the extra yard to provide value for money. Yes, it's frustrating for everyone, but this way you're in it together.

As well as maintaining lines of communication, I put a lot of effort into producing video content. I hosted a series of chats with fighters on Instagram Live, which was really about keeping fans interested and engaged. At the same time, we were effectively inviting people into our houses. There we were all dressed down, with bad hair and dim lighting, but that made it more relatable. We're all normal people with family and friends, and that emotion proved so valuable at this time.

I didn't restrict myself to talking about boxing either. Personal tools that can improve our lives like mindset and positivity are so important to me. I like talking about how we can improve our lives, and sometimes used my platform to share it. It may be as a result of this, but I have always received a lot of messages from people who are struggling, either personally or with their business, and I try to answer as many as I can. I'm not trying to win another customer here. I never thought in a million years I'd be in this position, but it comes with responsibility. It's still communication, however, and at a time of isolation that proved to be a lifeline for all sorts of reasons.

Shortly after I noticed that local restaurant shut its doors, just as lockdown kicked in, I received a flyer through my door. It was from the other restaurant across the road, and effectively a call to arms. *Our menu continues*, it said, *and we invite you to try our new takeaway service.* They offered a discount, a loyalty system, and basically told me this was one business that refused to lie down and die. While its competitor was sulking, they had seized the initiative and adapted to the situation.

I found the restaurant on social media, and watched with interest as they evolved the takeaway into a delivery service, hosted themed nights and even a Zoom quiz for customers, promising a bottle of wine or a few beers to any customers who took part. The creativity and energy that went into that reinvention was inspiring. It picked up traction, and I imagine at the end of their trading quarter those guys looked at their figures and saw that they'd done okay. They might even have increased their takings.

Meanwhile the restaurant opposite literally gathered dust. Any customers who once enjoyed eating there had probably given up and got their food from the place across the road.

This was a lesson in taking responsibility for your business. In many ways, the pandemic presented an opportunity to level the playing field and even seize the advantage. All of a sudden, if things hadn't been going well, you had a chance to shake things up. The challenges were enormous, but with the right mindset, it was also possible to be successful.

A week before that restaurant flyer dropped through my door, I set about launching my own response to the pandemic. There was no way I planned to hide and mooch about because we couldn't stage our fights. We were never going to pull the shutters on Matchroom. My next step was to consider our partners, from the sponsors to the broadcasters, and ask: what kind of content we could create? The big shows had been paused, but that air time needed filling and I wanted to be the one to do it.

We talked about repackaging classic fights, but it didn't feel fresh. At the same time, with talk of a lockdown growing, it looked highly likely that everyone was about to be stuck at home with all gyms and leisure centres shut. So, I began to think about what people would do for exercise, which gave me an idea.

With time fast running out to act, I picked up the phone to Sky Sports. They had seen all their live events cancelled, including the boxing, which meant they had a schedule to fill. So when I pitched them a proposal for a series that would require filming to begin immediately, it was a question of are you in or out?

With the green light, Matchroom then hired a TV production crew at short notice and invited a steady stream of celebrities, athletes and musicians to join us in the grounds of our headquarters. There, across the course of three long days, we set about filming thirty half-hour-long episodes of a show we called *Fighting Fit*. This was motivational viewing for people at home, encouraging them to get off the sofa and join in with familiar figures as expert trainers put them through their paces.

At this point, with more bad news coming out every day, people were nervous about shooting indoors. Even though we were in March, the weather was on our side. That's why I made the decision to use the grounds at Matchroom. It was green, spacious, had a rolling view of the capital's skyline and crucially kept everyone in the open air. Filming was intense. We needed to record ten episodes each day and it was literally a production line.

When someone pulled out, the producer turned to me and said, 'Eddie, get your shorts on.' It was embarrassing, but had to be done. The whole thing was frantic, but everyone committed 110 per cent. All I could think was *keep working and get through these three days*, and we did not stop until the final episode was in the can.

We wrapped on the Saturday. On the Monday, Boris Johnson went on TV and announced a nationwide lockdown. I sat back and thought, *We've done it!*

Matchroom had responded to the crisis creatively and kept our presence in the public eye. It was a big win for us in terms of positivity, because my team had risen to the challenge. A crisis had struck our business, but we didn't drop the shutters. With *Fighting Fit*, along with the dialogue we maintained across our social media channels, we forged new ways to connect. We'd made some money, too, but that wasn't so important. It was a stepping stone towards a bigger target I'd set myself before the pandemic struck.

The Pursuit of Opportunity

With lockdown in place, I began to see it not as a nightmare but as a test. For the first time since I started my career, I paused for breath. When I should've been on a plane, I was at home with the family. It gave me a chance to reflect on things and appreciate what I had achieved through the years. I hadn't completed everything I had planned for boxing, but I wondered whether I was at a stage in my life where I could've fallen into the mindset that has always terrified me. I was still pushing to go further than my dad, but frankly, I knew what I was doing now. It meant the sense of danger I once felt wasn't quite the force it was.

With age, experience and success, was I in danger of becoming complacent? Would I ever be able to return to the rat race with such intensity?

Even thinking that I might sit back came as a jolt to me. There was no way that I could allow it, and now here we were in the middle of a pandemic. All sporting events had been put on hold. The prospect of staging an arena fight in front of a huge crowd was out of the question. It presented a whole raft of challenges that nobody had anticipated.

And that excited me.

Just as we had pulled *Fighting Fit* out of the bag, I knew we could do the same thing with boxing. My main driver was the fact that I didn't think anyone else would be able to do it. I wasn't sure how, but my motivation to devise a solution was stronger than ever before. On social media, I promised that I would find a way. Some of the responses came back saying, 'You are relentless. Next level!' and that really pumped the blood through my veins.

It was exciting. If things had become easy for me, this was an opportunity for me to step up and see what I was really made from. I'd had a good ten years. Now here was a chance to prove it wasn't a fluke.

Every business is different, of course, but potentially at that moment in time we all faced a massive event. Those that stepped up and sought ways to adapt – and even reinvent – would survive and even thrive. I was determined to be among that number.

We had been blessed with really good weather while filming *Fighting Fit*. I'd barely had time to blink during the schedule, but remember thinking how lucky we were to have this location on our doorsteps. With a handsome mansion behind us, and a cracking view of the city skyline in the distance, I started wondering what else we could film here. It was an asset I looked out on every single day, but had never seen it in this context.

With arena shows out of the question, and even hangars and studios creating social distancing issues, I wandered out onto the grounds one day and imagined the possibilities. I knew our competitors would be touring studios with a view to staging a fight, and facing exactly the same barriers as us. This was literally a breath of fresh air, and in keeping with Matchroom's vision to be innovative and a cut above the rest. So, I went to see my old man.

'We can stage a fight in our garden,' I told him.

'What the fuck, Eddie?'

'We'll put up a ring, a canopy, create a TV studio on the balcony and host a summer of open-air shows. We'll have drones overhead to film every moment, fireworks . . . it'll be huge!'

When the rest of the team learned of my plans, the questions started coming. What about accommodation? Testing? Government regulations? The British Boxing Board of Control? Where will the press conference be held? How will it look without an audience? How will it *sound*? From that moment on it was a question of addressing each issue in turn . . . tick, tick, tick. Some I could deal with immediately, others would take days, weeks and even months, but once I had that vision in my head, I knew that it would become a reality.

I knew the risks we were running. At any time, in the midst of a global pandemic, all manner of factors beyond our control could bring the whole thing crashing down. That was no reason to walk away from it, however. We had a marathon to run like no other, and once I'd sold it to the team, we were united.

Matchroom would bring boxing back in a way that nobody could have imagined months earlier. With a ring under the heavens and exposed to the elements, *Fight Camp* would be a month-long spectacular that no fan could afford to miss.

Both timing and speed were critical. Like any company, we had to adapt and fast, while placing our reputation and value for money at the forefront. It was no easy task, and I thrived on it. I had to secure four night's worth of fights as early as possible, so the boxers could train. At the same time, I needed to sell the idea to our broadcast partners. I was well aware that every major sport would be looking to come back somehow, from the Premiership to Formula 1, and while the TV schedules were gathering dust, everyone would soon be scrapping for attention.

It meant I had to be completely serious about our intentions, grabbing attention while providing evidence and assurance that we were Covid-safe at every stage. Everyone involved needed to be comfortable in order for us to proceed. That wasn't a requirement to satisfy others – I had a duty to protect the welfare of every single person who saw *Fight Camp* as a solution to a massive problem faced by the boxing community.

With every day that passed, I could never say with complete confidence that we would reach that finish line. There were so many external factors I could not control, and yet we pressed onwards. Had I come up with this idea and dismissed it as too difficult or risky, then I wouldn't deserve to be here. It would be like the window cleaner who switches off his phone and says, 'We'll be back when we're back,' because to be honest, they might as well hand over their customers to the rival window cleaner who's up to the challenge.

It wasn't easy for me. It was fucking hard at times, the team and I were constantly demonstrating the strength of our health and safety policies to prove that we could do this. It was a necessary process, and it rightly tested our plans to be sure we had covered everything.

Quite simply, I was not prepared to fail. I didn't want to say I'd tried hard. It had to be a success, and the fact that I drove it with passion meant every milestone made me stronger. If anyone doubted I could do it, and there were voices, I became even more determined. I was selling my heart out to win them over, but above all I believed in the product. A fight under the stars, an incredible backdrop, the kind of lightshow and camerawork you'd normally expect from a Hollywood blockbuster, and a chance to hear every punch and groan of the boxers. Yes, it would be different, but also exciting beyond measure.

'That's all very well, Ed,' someone would say, 'but what if there's a storm?'

'Then it will look fucking epic.'

'But wouldn't it be safer to film this inside?'

'Surrounded by empty seats? Who wants to be reminded of the one thing that's missing? Let's give them fireworks, an incredible light show. Let's do things different, because other people wouldn't dare, and that's what Matchroom is all about!'

With the strategy in place to stage the show, I turned my attention to selling the story. The fans were engaged, because this was something that had never been attempted before in boxing, but I also had a running narrative to build. I wanted updates from the camp, with interviews and a behind-the-scenes documentary from the bubble to bring people into the heart of it all. Even testing was a point of interest, I realised, because no fight could take place without clean results. Engagement is key in any business venture, and in many ways there was more meat on the bones of this show than most.

In the build-up to *Fight Camp*, I was across social media night and day with news, views, opinions and debates. This was boxing gone hyperreal. With microphones around the ring and in each corner, fans could expect the raw brutality of each fight to come through the screens and into their living rooms. I guaranteed an intense experience, and when fans responded with such positivity, I shared their excitement.

Had I been the window cleaner, hungry to find a way through it all, you'd have been hearing from me constantly. Even if restrictions meant I couldn't visit your house and get up a ladder, I'd be providing updates and discounts you could expect from advance booking, because demand would be sky high once government guidelines relaxed. That kind of proactive thinking takes you places at challenging times. Whether you're cleaning windows, running a restaurant or hosting a world-class sporting event, let your market know that you're still in business – and bring them along for the ride.

It's safe to say I was fired up by everything about *Fight Camp*. It was the challenges, the freshness, the sheer ambition and near-impossibility of the whole venture that made it so exciting. I had chosen the hard route to bring back boxing, because in decades to come, I wanted to look back and say, 'Do you remember when we staged that World Title fight in the garden?' Even now, the craziness at the heart of that statement gets my adrenalin pumping.

I do believe that disruption can be healthy for business. The social changes caused by the pandemic have shaken us all to the core. Sadly, some sectors will struggle, but there will always be the opportunity to reflect, adapt and even thrive. For me, it was a chance to think deeply about the customs and conventions behind boxing promotion and ask what could be improved. With the competition hiding at home, I had a blank canvas to try to do things better, not for my sake but for everyone involved.

In putting *Fight Camp* together, I encouraged boxers to take the fight that would make compelling viewing. Rather than seeking to thread the easiest route to a title, which any good manager, trainer or agent might urge them to do, I felt we owed it to the fans to deliver clashes that would prove to be memorable. With no other fights scheduled for broadcast, I had boxers practically hammering down my door trying to get on the bill.

That allowed me to put fights together that fans were clamouring to see, like Sam Eggington v Ted Cheeseman; the much anticipated rematch between Katie Taylor and Delfine Persoon for the undisputed World Lightweight Titles; and of course, the heavyweight clash on the final night between Dillian Whyte and Alexander Povetkin. On paper, these were proper fights delivering quality entertainment for both broadcasters and fans. Whatever the outcome in the ring, it was a win for everyone in the face of adversity.

At this challenging and uncertain time, value for money is key. It applies to every business, no matter what the sector. Combined with innovation, in a bid to adapt to the changing circumstances, you have a spearhead for a strategy that could see you through to the other side. Ultimately, it's a question of doing whatever it takes so you're in good shape to come back stronger and better than ever.

Full Tilt for the Future

People often ask me if I enjoy watching a fight. Without doubt, I'm passionate about the sport. I love selling the story as it unfolds, with all the twists and turns, so that everyone from the fans to our broadcasting and sponsorship partners share my enthusiasm. From nailing down a deal that brings two big fighters into the ring, in a showdown everyone wants to see, to working on selling out a stadium event and hosting the press conferences, I am a businessman at heart who is committed to staging a show nobody will forget.

But when I finally settle in my ringside seat, as the referee brings the boxers out of their corners, I am purely a fan. All the selling and the showmanship, as well as the politics, are over. There is nothing more I can do now, but also I am emotionally invested in these fighters. I know them, and consider many to be close friends. Sometimes it's like watching a mate up there, and I'm desperate for them to win.

Some might say this is the finish line. Having run a marathon to make this show happen, at the size and scale that I promised from the outset, it should be a moment of glory for me. It never works out that way, though. I can get lost in the fight like I'm fifteen years old all over again, but I don't look around and think, *I've cracked it.*

When AJ faced Klitschko at Wembley Stadium in 2017, getting off the canvas to stop him late, we had 90,000 people in attendance. It was the biggest fight in British boxing history. Even so, I barely remember it. People would come up to me for a long time afterwards to ask what was going through my mind. I cannot say that I registered the scale of it or patted myself on the back, and I do wonder why I take it in my stride.

Maybe it goes back to my upbringing. On his regular walks around the grounds of his home, my old man is like a lost boy in paradise. He appreciates what he has, because he came from absolutely nothing, while my early memories include watching Steve Davis and Chris Eubank win world titles. I feel a bit sad when I think like that, but it also drives me to embrace what I've been given and take it further than my dad could ever imagine.

Naturally I celebrate with my fighters when they win. It can be a massively emotional moment, and I'm often first through the ropes to congratulate them. As the ring fills, however, I'm quickly back into the role of promoter. Someone with a microphone will hustle for my attention, and suddenly I'm giving an interview for television or radio. The questions start flowing and before the winner has even lifted the belt, I'm being asked about their next fight. Even as I'm responding, planting the seed for the next story, my mobile will be buzzing with messages from agents or managers hoping to start talks at the earliest opportunity.

It's relentless, and I wouldn't have it any other way.

*

So, we've come to the end of the book. I really hope you enjoyed it. I almost feel like I've had a mini-counselling session reading this back, but it's helped me reflect on the past and has made me motivated for the future. So good luck to you, my friends – work hard, look after your family, and follow your dreams. But most of all, I hope you find happiness in everything you do.

ROUND 12 – KEY TAKEAWAYS

- In the pursuit of success, you have to be prepared to deal with tough times, but when you feel like quitting, remember why you started. You must stay calm, take a deep breath and solve the immediate short-term problems that are in front of you. If you simply freeze or don't react fast enough, then the hole may deepen.

- The worst thing you can do as a business is to go quiet, you must always communicate with your customer. It just creates anxiety and distrust, and you lose all the qualities of a vital bond. Jeff Bezos, CEO of Amazon, said, 'Focusing on the customer makes a company more resilient,' and I couldn't agree more. The last thing you want to do is run away from the problem. It's a basic fundamental. Even if you don't have any instant answers, make yourself available to your customer and bring them on your journey. Don't hide.

- In all times, we must be relentless in our pursuit of perfection – it's a recurring theme to success. So wherever you are right now and whatever your future holds, never let yourself be outworked by the competition.